Stupid Christmas

Other Books by Leland Gregory

Stupid Christmas

LELAND GREGORY

Andrews McMeel
Publishing, LLC
Kansas City • Sydney • London

ISBN-13: 978-0-7407-9953-2
ISBN-10: 0-7407-9953-3

Library of Congress Control Number: 2010924513

10 11 12 13 14 RR2 10 9 8 7 6 5 4 3 2 1

www.andrewsmcmeel.com

Attention: Schools and Businesses

Andrews McMeel books are available at quantity discounts with bulk
purchase for educational, business, or sales promotional use. For information,
please write to: Special Sales Department, Andrews McMeel Publishing, LLC,
1130 Walnut Street, Kansas City, Missouri 64106.

Stupid Christmas

Christmas Around the World

In a number of European countries, it isn't Santa Claus who punishes "naughty" kids with coal and twigs—the job of identifying the "not nice" is left to centuries-old, and very unpleasant, characters. According to a series of articles from the December 2008 issue of the German magazine *Der Spiegel*, the extremely ugly witch La Befana terrifies Italian children and is capable of flying her broomstick into the house of bad kids through keyholes. In Austria and Croatia, children are terrified of Krampus, a horned, devil-like character with a long tongue and the head of a goat, who beats the misbehaving with a stick of birch. And in the folklore of Germany there is Knecht Ruprecht, which translates as "Farmhand Rupert" or "Servant Rupert." He makes children perform a song or dance for Saint Nicholas to prove they are good. If they are, they receive a gift. . . . If not, they are beaten soundly by Servant Ruprecht.

Mr. Obsession

Andy Park was bored and depressed on July 14, 1994, so he put up some Christmas decorations, fixed a traditional Christmas meal, popped open a bottle of Moët champagne, and suddenly felt better. So every day since then, Mr. Park has celebrated Christmas. He estimates that he has ingested nearly 118,000 sprouts, hundreds of thousands of mince pies, around 5,000 bottles of champagne, and enough turkeys to shut down a turkey ranch. The economy has caused Mr. Christmas to cut back on his daily celebrations, but he still finds time to watch the Queen's Christmas Message on video every day. In an article in the December 14, 2009, edition of *Metro*, Park, from Melksham, Wiltshire, in England, said, "Before the credit crunch I was eating a 14 pound turkey, now I'm down to a four pounder. . . . From 40 mince pies a day I've gone to 12."

Dung Goes the Christmas Bell

The traditional Christmas Nativity scene consists of Mary, Joseph, the Three Wise Men, Baby Jesus, a shepherd or two, and some animals. But for three centuries, in northeast Spain's Catalonia region, there has been another character lurking in the crèche, a "caganer." The caganer—literally, "pooper"—is an icon portrayed with its pants pulled down answering a call a nature. The exact origin of the caganer is lost, but the character, used since the seventeenth century, is usually tucked away from the other characters and is also used as a "search and find" game for the children.

On Christmas Day, 1868, President Andrew Johnson's last significant act was granting unconditional amnesty to all Confederate soldiers for their actions in the Civil War. Confederate president Jefferson Davis declined to accept it.

Dazed and Confused

Santa Claus is coming to Raleigh, North Carolina, but Mrs. Claus isn't welcomed there anymore. The Greater Raleigh Merchants Association, which sponsors the city's Christmas parade, banned Mrs. Claus from appearing in the traditional red suit and hat because, said executive director John Odom, it would be "confusing for the children." According to a November 21, 2009, article in the *Raleigh News & Observer*, the association went so far as to require that only Santa could wear the infamous red Santa-style hat, and even discouraged spectators from wearing the hat, so the children wouldn't have any problem identifying the real Santa.

Equal Access

The Nativity scene at Chambersburg, Pennsylvania's Memorial Fountain and Statue has been a town tradition for years. The legal doctrine that allows public religious displays also denotes that every religion is welcome to exhibit equally. So in 2009 the Pennsylvania Nonbelievers informed the town that it was going to display a sign reading "Celebrating Solstice—Honoring Atheist War Veterans." Before the sign went up, the law came down. "The downside of 'everything' is it means everything," explained Bill McLaughlin, president of the borough's council. From now on no decorations will be allowed on city property.

In November 1939, during the Great Depression, Franklin D. Roosevelt ordered Thanksgiving be celebrated one week earlier than usual, thereby extending the Christmas shopping season.

Good Grief

In 2009, when a speech by President Barack Obama preempted the annual telecast of the 1965 classic *A Charlie Brown Christmas*, the mayor of Arlington, Tennessee, Russell Wiseman, really could have used his security blanket. The mayor wrote on Facebook that the interruption was "total crap," and saying that "our muslim president" had "deliberately timed" his political telecast to interrupt the religious message of *Peanuts*. Wiseman also posted, "you obama people need to move to a muslim country . . . oh wait, that's America . . . pitiful" and "you know, our forefathers had it written in the original Constitution that ONLY property owners could vote, if that has stayed in there, things would be different." He later apologized for his "blockhead" remarks and claimed that it was his poorly executed attempt at tongue-in-cheek humor. I guess Russell Wiseman won't ever be confused for one of the Three Wise Men.

Faux Fir

Citing safety concerns, the town of Poole in Dorset, England, decided not to purchase their traditional Norway fir Christmas tree. "If it blows over and kills someone then somebody is liable for it," said Richard Randall-Jones of the Town Center Management Board. Instead, they opted for a fake tree that cost more than $22,500. "Even better," said Randall-Jones, the pretend tree had "no decorations for drunken teenagers to steal." The town's citizens, however, hated the thirty-three-foot "traffic cone," and some protestors ripped chunks of the tree's "Astroturf" away, exposing its metal frame. According to a November 27, 2009, article in the *Times*, the Management Board heeded the public outcry and replaced the fake with a real tree.

Oh, Little Town of Santa Claus

It's called "The City That Loves Children" and is complete with streets with names such as Candy Cane Lane, Reindeer Street, Dancer Street, Prancer Street, Sleigh Street, and Rudolph Way. Santa Claus, Georgia, is a tiny (0.2 square miles), thinly populated (with approximately 250 residents) town whose city hall is located at 25 December Drive. A December 21, 2009, article in the *Macon (GA) Telegraph* reported that the residents aren't overly jolly and they don't celebrate Christmas year-round; it's just your typical small southern town with endearing street names. The town was incorporated in 1941 as a ploy to sell locally grown pecans, but they're always happy to postmark your Christmas cards.

It's the Thought That Counts

Misty Ann Lumsden, of Kelso, Washington, was arrested after allegedly stealing $794 in merchandise from a Walmart store in nearby Longview. Lumsden told officers she made four trips in and out of the store over a two-hour period, stashing the stolen items along a fence. She explained to the arresting officers that she stole the merchandise to give to her child as Christmas presents. According to a December 24, 2009, article in the *Longview Daily News*, among the stolen items were alcoholic beverages, condoms, and adult-sized clothing.

Three days later, Kelso police arrested Lumsden again at the Three Rivers Mall in Kelso and charged her with two counts of third-degree theft and one count of marijuana possession.

They Stuck in Their Thumb

The management at R.F. Brookes, a frozen pizza base making plant in Wigston, Leicestershire, in England, wanted to thank their five hundred member strong workforce for their dedication and gave everyone a Christmas pudding in December 2009. But the sweet treat turned sour when the employees noticed that the expiration date on the puddings was March 2009. Although management explained in a letter that the puddings had been tested by food technicians and would be fine to eat until January they quickly ordered new ones and apologized after several employees complained to the media.

Mince Pie Charts

According to a September 4, 2007, article in London's *Daily Mail*, congregants of Reverend Tom Ambrose of Saint Mary and Saint Michael Church in Trumpington, Cambridge, met to voice their complaints about the vicar. Most of the people in attendance didn't like that Ambrose conducted several Christmas sermons using Microsoft's PowerPoint software.

In the original printing of the poem "A Visit from Saint Nicholas" in 1823, the last two reindeer were named "Dunder and Blixem," which are very close to the Dutch words for thunder and lightning, *donder* and *bliksem*. "Blixem" is an alternative spelling for *bliksem* but "dunder" is not an accepted alternative spelling for *donder*. It is quite possible that there was a minor printing error and Dunder's name should have been Donder.

Don't Wine About It

In a November 2, 2007, article in *Der Spiegel*, Catholic priests in Ireland and Northern Ireland expressed concern about their respective governments' proposals to lower the blood-alcohol level for driving while impaired from .08 to .05. The priests complained that because of a shortage of available priests, they were required to drive greater distances to conduct Masses for the upcoming Christmas season. And, they reminded authorities, as they are obliged to drink any leftover sacramental wine from every Mass they conduct, there would be the distinct probability that they could exceed the newly enacted blood-alcohol level.

Just Reindeer Games

John Hayes, a middle school coach from Marietta, Georgia, was arrested in December 2007 and charged with criminal trespass for unlawful purposes, contributing to the delinquency of minors, and reckless conduct after he drove a group of his students around in his pickup truck at night so they could vandalize a number of Christmas decorations. Inflatables were deflated and displays were damaged and in one case, according to a report from WGCL-TV in Atlanta, two plastic reindeer were left entangled in a "sexual position."

Even though smoke was billowing out of the store, firefighters in Mentor, Ohio, had to physically restrain a number of enthusiastic Christmas shoppers from continuing to enter the Dillard's at Great Lakes Mall during a December 6, 2006, electrical fire.

They Even Took the Roast Beast

In 2009, Louisville, Kentucky's annual Christmas celebration, Light Up Louisville, was supposed to have a *How the Grinch Stole Christmas* theme. But then a modern Grinch showed up—a lawyer. Dr. Seuss Enterprises in San Diego got wind of the celebration and sent a lawyer down from Mount Crumpit to explain copyright infringement to all the Lous in Louisville. The Louisville Convention and Visitors Bureau agreed to alter certain aspects of the parade and to drop the costume character of the Grinch all together. "The three words that best describe this legal action are as follows, and I quote, 'Stink, 'Stank,' 'Stunk!'" said Jim Wood, chief executive officer of the Louisville Convention and Visitors Bureau.

Merry Hanukkah!

According to a November 28, 2008, article in the Arutz Sheva (Israel National News), the Bush administration sent out postcards to Jewish leaders in the United States inviting them to the White House for a Hanukkah reception. The card, however, showed a horse-drawn cart pulling a Christmas tree to the White House and alternatively outraged and amused many in the Jewish community. Spokesperson Sally McDonough blamed a "staff mistake" for the gaffe, noting "it is just something that fell through the cracks."

What the . . . ?

A public library in Oberlin, Ohio, unveiled a holiday display by conceptual artist Keith McGuckin that featured a legless Santa Claus in a wheelchair being pushed down the stairs by an evil Christmas tree. A narrative that accompanied the image explained that Santa had lost his legs when they got entangled in power lines during an alcoholic binge and that the sadistic tree is planning on stealing the money in the Salvation Army kettle and visiting a strip club. A December 4, 2008, article from United Press International quoted library director Darren McDonough as saying that the display would remain in place during the holiday season and to "Remember the old library saying—'If we don't have something to offend you, we're not doing our job.'"

Looking a Gift Horse in the Mouth

On November 23, 2008, fifty-nine-year-old Robert E. Dendy stopped by police headquarters in Tonawanda, New York, wished the officers on duty a Merry Christmas, and presented them with a Christmas wreath. Knowing Dendy's recent criminal past, the officers contacted the store next door that sold the wreaths and found out that the wreath had been stolen. According to the *Tonawanda News*, Dendy admitted to the theft and was arrested.

Sending red Christmas cards to anyone in Japan constitutes bad etiquette, since funeral notices there are customarily printed in red.

Up on the Roof Top
Click, Click, Click

Little Cindy Lou Who finding the Grinch in her house was nothing compared to the Christmas visitor spotted by a neighbor in Vancouver, British Columbia. Santa Claus, complete with beard and red suit, was toting a shotgun instead of a bag of goodies and was seen sneaking into a house with two accomplices. The neighbor quickly called 911 to report that this appearance of Santa a few days before Christmas 1997 gave him "clause" for concern. Sirens on the police cars apparently frightened away the jolly fat man and his two elves—but not before they had tied up the occupants of the house and ransacked the place. Police soon discovered why Santa had made his little visit: The house had an elaborate marijuana-growing operation in the basement. I always wondered what Santa had in that little pipe.

It Came Upon
a Midnight Clear

Lonnie Williams had fallen on hard times. His wife had died a year before and he and his two daughters had moved from New York to North Carolina so he could look for a job. He couldn't find one. Now, living in a strange place in 1991, Williams was homeless and jobless, and to make matters worse, it was Christmas Eve. He didn't know what to do. A friend suggested he call 911—and that's what he did. The 911 operator listened to Williams's story and then referred him to Shelby Police Department dispatcher Ray Digh. "He was incredibly nice," Williams said. "He said, 'Don't worry, we'll find something.'" Digh got on the police radio and at 11:30 p.m. sent out a message to other police officers. Soon, the donations came pouring in: new, wrapped presents, toys, games, and money. By 1 A.M. Christmas Day, Digh, city and county police officers, and even Santa Claus (played by a Shelby city worker) delivered the Christmas gifts to Tiffany and Kenyada. "It was an excellent Christmas for me, and also for the girls. I didn't have anything for them," said Williams.

I Said, "Flock the Tree!"

According to a Manatee County, Florida, sheriff's report, the mother of thirty-seven-year-old Thomas Edward Lackie called police to report that her son had attacked his father. Apparently Lackie had assaulted his father by throwing a three-foot Christmas tree at him. When he realized he had missed, he picked up the five-pound base and tried to hit him with that before his parents restrained him. Lackie was charged with felony assault. No motive was reported in the December 3, 2008, article in the *Sarasota Herald-Tribune*.

GPS:
God's Positioning System

I think it's because Jesus is small enough to take," said John Bonde, director of operations for Wellington, Florida. "Everything else is too big." That's why the town has outfitted their Nativity scene figurines with GPS tracking devices, the *Palm Beach Post* reported on December 13, 2008. The previous year, an eighteen-year-old woman snatched Jesus but was quickly tracked down because of the device. She was originally charged with felony theft, but the town dropped the charges so the woman could join the U.S. Marine Corps.

The Cane Mutiny

A small backyard gathering in Del Paso Heights in Sacramento, California, was interrupted when an apparently intoxicated neighbor, forty-nine-year-old Donald Kercell, crashed the party. Kercell attacked several guests before one unnamed partygoer fought back with the only weapon at hand: a two-foot-tall Christmas candy cane lawn decoration. According to a November 28, 2009, article in the *Sacramento Bee*, the Candy Man knocked the knife out of Kercell's hand and subdued him until police arrived. Kercell was charged with assault with a deadly weapon, but the reason for his rampage was unknown. The man who gave Kercell a canning was not charged as he was acting in self-defense.

In 1995, officials in Belfast debated over whom they should invite to light the city's official Christmas tree: President Clinton or the Mighty Morphin Power Rangers.

Trees a Crowd

Bren Knox of Trinity, North Carolina, has sixty-one Christmas trees in her house, each decorated with a different theme. Knox told WFMY-TV on December 16, 2008, that she started the collection eleven years before when her daughter wanted a separate Christmas tree in her room while Knox was out of town on business. From there, said Knox, her family trees kept multiplying. "When people hear how many trees I have in my home, they think I'm crazy," the mother of two said. Knox occasionally offers an open house to collect canned food items that she then donates to the Salvation Army.

Rudolph Wept

Artist Jimmy Wright was tired of the commercialization of Christmas and wanted to "stop the orgy of consumption." So he erected a cross and crucified . . . Santa Claus. Wright, who lives in Metchosin, on Vancouver Island in British Columbia, titled the piece *Sumptum Fac Donec Consumptus Sis*, which, Wright says, translates to "Shop Till You Drop." Several neighbors and even the pastor of Saint Mary's Anglican Church asked Wright to remove the effigy, but he refused, stating that Santa "represents frivolous consumption. He shot Jesus right out of the saddle." According to a December 7, 2006, article in Victoria's *Times Colonist*, Wright's "orgy of consumption" didn't include him. "It's a funny feeling when I'm sitting in my hot tub, looking out this way," said Wright. "And I'm trying to make a statement to everybody to slow down on what they can consume, and I'm in a 6,400-square-foot home."

Watch Your Mouth

In some cases the little kids can get a little bit scared," confirms national operations manager Glen Jansz of Westaff, the Australian firm that recruits seasonal Santa Clauses. As reported in the November 11, 2007, edition of Melbourne, Victoria's *Herald Sun*, current training sessions urge temporary Santas to eliminate or "tone down" the "Ho, ho, ho" laugh and instead replace it "Ha, ha, ha." Jansz said that the traditional laugh can come off as a little frightening and might be considered derogatory to women, as "ho" is slang for prostitutes.

According to a December 6, 2007, article in the *Vancouver (BC) Province*, Westaff fired seventy-year-old John Oakes for saying "ho, ho, ho" and for singing "Jingle Bells."

A Shot in the Dark

It was a gift that he went from hating to loving. Store owner Leon Wilson's wife had given him a motion-activated singing Christmas tree and placed it near his cash register. Every time someone came into the store the tree's eyes would pop open, its mouth would move, and it would call out "Merry Christmas, Everybody!" and sing "Jingle Bells." According to a January 5, 1999, Reuters article, Wilson's Baton Rouge, Louisiana, store had been robbed twice in the previous week so he had taken to sleeping in the store. In the early morning he was awakened by the singing tree and saw two boys holding a crowbar by his cash register. "They spotted me and bolted for the door, and I started shooting, aiming low cause I didn't want to kill them," Wilson said. Baton Rouge police said the two sixteen-year-old suspects, one with a minor leg wound and the other with buckshot in his buttocks, were arrested on burglary charges and released to their parents.

There's a New Grinch in Town

Lisa Jensen, wanting to "put a message of peace out there," hung a Christmas wreath in the shape of a peace sign on the outside wall of her home in Pagosa Springs, Colorado. But Bob Kearns, president of the Loma Linda Homeowners Association said, "The peace sign has a lot of negativity associated with it. It's also an anti-Christ sign. That's how it started." He also claimed that the subdivision's rules state that "signs, billboards or advertising structures of any kind" are banned, and subject to a $25-per-day fine. Jensen, a past association president, estimated that her fine would be close to $1,000 but doubts they could force her to pay. Kearns ordered the architectural control committee to require Jensen to remove the wreath, but according to a November 26, 2006, Associated Press article, members refused after concluding that it was merely a seasonal symbol that didn't say anything. Kearns fired all five committee members.

It's the Thought That Counts

The city of New London, Connecticut, wanted to seize, by "eminent domain," 115 privately held homes to develop condos, shops, and hotels to create jobs and stimulate the economy. One woman, Susette Kelo, fought the project and carried her case all the way to the Supreme Court, which sided with the city. Meanwhile, the city raised the buyout price on her home from $123,000 to $442,155, and started eviction procedures in June 2006. But Kelo had the last word, actually the last rhyming words, as she sent Christmas cards to many of the politicians involved in the taking of her property. As reported in the December 20, 2006, edition of *New London Day*, the card showed her seized property and included a poem that read, in part:

> *Here is my house that you did take*
> *From me to you, this spell I make*
> *Your houses, your homes*
> *Your family, your friends*
> *May they live in misery*
> *That never ends*
> *I curse you all*
> *May you rot in hell*
> *To each of you*
> *I send this spell.*

One supporter of the project, Gail Schwenker-Mayer, who received one of Kelo's cards, said, "[It's] amazing anyone could be so vindictive when they've made so much money."

Good Vibrations

The fact that there's sand in the desert and there's also sand on the beach must have been the inspiration behind the 2006 Christmas Nativity play at Saint Stephen's Church in Tonbridge, Kent, in England, because the traditional music was replaced with music from the Beach Boys. On December 22, 2006, Agence France-Presse reported that in the performance, Mary turned into a "little surfer girl" to sing "God Only Knows." The Three Wise Men, portrayed as Brian, Carl, and Dennis Wilson, performed such favorites as "Fun, Fun, Fun" and "Good Vibrations." Said youth pastor Jim Prestwood, "We were fed up with the Nativity plays. . . . They are nice but they can just be a bit dull. It made it a bit more realistic, a bit more attractive to people."

Clement Clarke Moore's famous poem is not called "The Night Before Christmas" but is actually titled "A Visit from Saint Nicholas."

His Bark Is Worse Than His Bite

The stockings were hung by the chimney with care, the tree was decorated, and the dog was about to vomit on the carpet. When ten-year-old John Roemer saw his nauseated dog, Pookie, about to puke, he rushed over and pushed the dog off the rug. Suddenly, the family's large artificial tree fell over, nearly crushing the little boy. So, keeping one eye on the cramping canine, John pushed the tree back into its stand and then moved back to look at his handiwork. That's when the tree fell again—this time pinning little John under it. He couldn't get up and the dog's cheeks were starting to puff out again. John was able to reach a cordless phone and called several neighbors to help him out from under the Christmas tree. Most weren't home in his Fremont, Nebraska, neighborhood and one "didn't believe me," said John. He finally dialed 911 and explained his situation. Emergency dispatchers have heard it all before, and they believed the boy was pinned by the pine. Police and firefighters freed the young boy, who wasn't hurt by the "Bonzi" tree.

Ho, Ho, What?

On Christmas morning, 1996, Scott Kane and his wife heard someone prowling around in their home in Chevy Chase, Maryland, and called 911. Despite the blaring sirens and screeching tires of several squad cars—and then seven police officers storming into the living room—twenty-three-year-old Roger Augusto Sosa, who had broken into the couple's home, was still sitting happily under the Kanes' Christmas tree opening their presents.

The Butt of the Law

The Maine Bureau of Liquor Enforcement reversed its decision to block the sale of Santa's Butt Winter Porter, a January 5, 2007, AP article reported. The label on the beer depicts a rear view of a Santa, sipping a beer and sitting on his butt on a "butt," a large barrel brewers once used to store beer. State officials originally banned the sale of the beer because of fears that the image on the label would attract children to drink the beer. But the state attorney general's office realized that the humorous label on the novelty brew is plainly protected by the First Amendment. Dan Shelton, owner of Shelton Brothers, who distributes the beer, said, "Minors are not going to be looking to buy beer because Santa Claus is on the label." If I'm not mistaken, regardless of what state we're talking about, minors can't buy beer anyway.

Something Else Grew Three Sizes That Day

A number of parents complained about a merchandising tie-in with Jim Carrey's 2000 live-action movie *How the Grinch Stole Christmas*. In question was a furry green Grinch doll that was sold to children. Its heart lit up when its belly was rubbed. The complaints were that it wasn't his belly that had to be rubbed; it was, in fact, his crotch. The toy was quickly pulled from store shelves.

Too Bad It's Not a Silent Night

Tom DuBois, a judge in Columbia, Tennessee, found a unique way of punishing people for minor crimes without sending them to jail: He made them sing for their sins. DuBois let minor traffic offenders off without a fine if they would stand up in court and sing a Christmas carol—which some claim were so bad they should have been a violation of the city's noise ordinance. According to a December 20, 2003, article in Nashville's *Tennessean*, DuBois's courtroom echoed with the off-keys sounds of "Jingle Bells," "Rudolph the Red-Nosed Reindeer," and "We Wish You a Merry Christmas." If the unmusical motorist was completely tone-deaf, court officer Kenny Lovett chimed in because he sang "in his church choir." DuBois also required a donation of five canned items to be given to the Second Harvest Food Bank.

Flue Flighters

'Twas the night before Christmas and . . . well, that's where the similarities end. Police extracted Joseph Hubbert from inside a narrow chimney of a bookstore on Christmas Eve. As reported in a December 27, 2003, *St. Paul Pioneer Press* article, police and fire rescuers could hardly contain their laughter as the criminal Kris Kringle was pulled from his claustrophobic confines. Even though he was arrested for burglary, Hubbert should consider himself lucky. Four years earlier, workers demolishing a building on the other side of town discovered a pair of sneakers poking out of a flue along with the dead body of another apparent robber.

White Christmas

In a raid on a warehouse used by Rio de Janeiro's most notorious narcotics gang, Comando Vermelho (Portuguese for "Red Command"), police discovered hundreds of freshly pressed copies of *Prohibited Rap,* a CD that the gang had intended as Christmas presents for their best customers. "It was the first time we had done anything like this," said gang member Samson, in a November 26, 1999, article in the *Boston Globe.* "It would have been a nice thank-you for our best customers, the ones who bought more than five bags of cocaine."

The sugarplums mentioned in the poem
"A Visit from Saint Nicholas" (and in Tchaikovsky's
"Nutcracker Suite") have nothing to do with plums.
They are actually hard candies.

The Fir Was Really Flying

Police in Pittsburgh, Pennsylvania, considered a charge of disorderly conduct for an unidentified thirty-one-year-old man who was too lazy to drag his Christmas tree down to the street for pickup and decided to simply toss it out his sixth-floor window on Christmas Day. According to a December 27, 1999, article in the *New York Times*, the discarded Douglas fir hit a power line on the way down, knocking out electricity to about four hundred customers for nearly an hour and briefly cutting off radio contact with police.

How Not to Return Christmas Gifts

Nassau County, New York, police arrested forty-four-year-old Vincent Festa at an Oyster Bay Radio Shack as he tried to return $2,198.93 of stolen electronics equipment. Store employees recognized Festa as the man who had stolen the items from them on December 21, 1999. Items included a desktop computer, MP3 player, digital camera, 2.5-inch television, home theater system, phone, and digital memory card. According to a December 29, 2004, article in the *New York Post*, employees called police, who arrested Festa while he was still in the store.

When What to My Wondering Eyes Should Appear . . .

It sounded like a call right out of Whoville. While driving around with his family looking at Christmas lights, a man spotted something on a neighbor's rooftop. It was Santa. But not your plastic Santa with a light in his belly—no, this Santa was frantically waving and shouting. Was he wishing everyone a Merry Christmas? Nope. He was begging someone to help him down. The passerby called 911, and the fire department helped the stranded Santa. Apparently Jolly Old Saint Nick wasn't so jolly after his ladder broke and he was stuck on the rooftop, click, click, click. Staying out in the winter wonderland for five hours gave this deserted do-gooder a mild case of frostbite on one toe. The paramedics soon realized that the rosy red cheeks weren't part of the outfit, either.

911 Is Not a Toy

An emergency situation is a relative thing. To some it means the possible loss of life and limb. To a five-year-old girl, however, it could mean her yo-yo broke. And three days before Christmas, 1999, that's just what happened to Emily Barg—that and the fact she was curious to see what would happen if she called 911. When the fire department showed up at her house she realized what the call would bring: trouble. Little Emily was lectured on the dangers of what she had done and made to promise she would never call again unless it was a real emergency.

Emily showed up at the fire station a few hours later to apologize in the best way she knew how—with a plate of homemade chocolate chip cookies and a note that read "I am very, very sorry. I baked these cookies for you. I hope you like them and you can forgive me. Now I am going to write a letter to Santa to tell him I am sorry, too." The firefighters accepted the little girl's apology and quickly gobbled down all the cookies.

I'll Keep an Eye Out for You

The ever-watchful eye of the surveillance camera or closed-circuit television has helped catch many a thief while plying their trade. And when fifty antique glass eyes went missing from the Owensboro Medical Health System in Kentucky, the videotape quickly helped identify the criminal. Police were baffled over why someone would steal glass eyes, as there isn't a high demand for them on the black market. But the most unusual fact about this Christmas Eve 2003 crime is the suspect's name. Are you ready? The person arrested for stealing fifty glass eyes was . . . Melissa Jane Wink.

He's Making a List and Checking It Twice

"A bottle comes flying through her door and immediately lights up her living room," said Hermosa Beach, California, police sergeant Paul Wolcott. "She was barely able to escape with her life." Wolcott was describing the aftermath of a Molotov cocktail thrown through a woman's glass front door, causing $200,000 in damages. Brandi Nicole Nason threw the gasoline bomb on Christmas Day 2003 into the home of her former stepmother because Nason was dissatisfied with a Christmas gift the woman had given her.

Charles Dickens's immortal character of Ebenezer Scrooge in *A Christmas Carol* blurts out the term "Bah, Humbug!" when referring to Christmas. It sounds nasty, but what does it mean? The word "humbug" is an archaic term meaning "hoax," "jest," or "fraud."

More Than Visions of Sugarplums

Here's a part of the Santa story that's hard to swallow. Apparently, Dr. Ian Edwards, the head of education at the Royal Botanic Gardens in Edinburgh, Scotland, theorized that it might not have been reindeer that helped Santa Claus fly but magic mushrooms. Dr. Edwards, reported the *Daily Telegraph* on January 14, 2002, held a seminar about the Sami people of Lapland, one of the oldest indigenous cultures in the world, whose stories tell that people used to feed hallucinogenic fungi to their herd of reindeer. Edwards said, "They used to feed red and white fly-agaric mushrooms to their reindeer, then drink the animals' urine. Drinking the urine would give them a high similar to taking LSD. One of the results was that they thought they and their reindeer were flying through space, looking down on the world." Edwards claimed that Santa's traditional red and white coat may have been inspired by the bright color of the mushroom.

Shopping Around for Trouble

Gardenia Zakrzewski Johansson pulled into the parking lot of the Neiman Marcus store in Scottsdale, Arizona, and gave the valet the keys to her BMW. Before she and her little dog went into the store, she asked the valet if he could keep an eye on something she left in the backseat: her two-year-old son. According to the December 12, 2006, *Mesa East Valley Tribune*, when Johansson emerged from the store thirty minutes later, with her shopping bag full, police were there to nab her. Johansson confessed she didn't know the name of the valet to whom she had given her keys but did remember he had "brown hair." The woman apologized for taking so long in the store but, she explained, her Christmas present wasn't wrapped, she needed to stop and get some cosmetics, and then she met an old friend and had a chat. It was then Johnasson's turn to ride in the backseat—of a squad car.

You're a Ho, Ho, Ho

Christmas is the busiest time of the year for the post office. People mail millions of boxes, cards, and letters to friends and relatives everywhere in the world. It's a happy time, a joyous time. So it came as some surprise to the good people of Ohio when twelve thousand pieces of mail were stamped with an unusual greeting of holiday cheer. Instead of a brightly stamped "Merry Christmas," the Yuletide mail recipients got a Scroogy "You Bitch" stamped on their mail, courtesy of their local post office. It gives the expression "ho, ho, ho" a whole new meaning.

Father Chris-Miss

A Santa Claus at a Walmart store in Louisville, Kentucky, was fired after several children noticed that "Father" Christmas had breasts. And they weren't fat man boobs, either—they were real, which is understandable because the store had hired Marta Brown, a woman. The store feared that a female Santa Claus would drive customers away, hurt business, and even damage its reputation. But Mama Christmas took her "discrimination" case to the Kentucky Commission on Human Rights, and is seeking $67,000 in lost wages and pain and suffering.

Cold, Harsh Cash

A week before Christmas 1777, George Washington and his Continental army established camp at Valley Forge, Pennsylvania, for the winter, remaining there until June 1778. It's true that as many as two thousand men died during those six months but it wasn't because of the weather. The close quarters were a breeding ground for typhus, typhoid, dysentery, and pneumonia, but the main killer was mismanagement and indifference. Pennsylvania farmers elected to sell their produce to the British instead of the newly found United States because they trusted the English sterling over the newly minted American money.

It's the Gift That Counts

Green Forest, Arkansas, police officer Tommy Hayden arrested a thirteen-year-old boy who allegedly threatened to cut off his mother's head with a butcher knife because he "had just discovered that she had not purchased him the [Christmas] present he had requested." The boy didn't cut his mother, but he did punch and kick her when she tried to disarm him. According to a December 26, 2004, AP article, the juvenile was taken to Carroll County Jail after admitting he threatened his mother's life and "said that all would have been well if she had just bought him the correct present."

As a joke, Andrew Jackson sent out formal invitations to the annual Christmas ball to a well-known mother-and-daughter prostitute team in Salisbury, North Carolina. No one thought it was particularly funny.

Secret Santa

M erry Christmas. Thank you for leaving your car door unlocked. Instead of stealing your car I gave you a present. Hopefully this will land in the hands of someone you love, for my love is gone now. Merry Christmas to you," read a typed note found on the front seat of a Boston, Massachusetts's man's car. But the most amazing thing about the note was that it was unsigned and was accompanied by a diamond engagement ring. Although he reported the incident to police, the man decided to keep the three diamond ring set in a white gold band after a jeweler appraised its value at $15,000.

Gangs of the North Pole

A group of men all dressed as Santa Claus went on a drunken rampage in Auckland, New Zealand. An estimated forty-five Father Christmases celebrating "Santarchy" vandalized Christmas trees and lawn ornaments, threw beer bottles at people and cars, shoplifted, and basically terrorized the town. In the *New Zealand Herald*, Alex Dyer, organizer of "Santarchy," said the Merry Mob was not, contrary to press reports, protesting the commercialization of Christmas. "It's not against anyone," he insisted. "We're just dressing up as Santa and getting drunk. We just like booze."

Dirty Santa

Fifty-two-year-old Richard Mullen was arrested and charged with disorderly conduct after he dropped his pants several times in a Salem, New Hampshire, mall. The *Manchester Union Leader* reported that Mullen, who was dressed as Santa Claus at the time, said he was "just having some fun with the kids." According to police captain Robert Larsen, Mullen would have been charged with indecent exposure except for the fact that he was wearing another pair of trousers under his Santa pants.

Dingell Bells, Dingell Bells

'Twas the week before Christmas and all through the House,
No bills were passed 'bout which FOX News could grouse;
Tax cuts for the wealthy were passed with great cheer,
So vacations in St. Barts soon would be near.

—Representative John Dingell (D-Michigan) bustin' a
rhyme on December 6, 2005, regarding House Resolution
579, which said the House of Representatives:

(1) recognizes the importance of the symbols and
traditions of Christmas;

(2) strongly disapproves of attempts to ban references to
Christmas; and

(3) expresses support for the use of these symbols and
traditions, for those who celebrate Christmas.

Ring in the Holidays

Being the very model of a modern mature woman, Janne Grim decided she would propose to her boyfriend as opposed to waiting for the traditional vice versa. The young Norwegian woman invited her boyfriend, Svein Froeytland, to a Christmas party and hid the wedding ring in his porridge. She watched impatiently as he wolfed down the porridge, but when he didn't mention the ring she took that as a "no." After swallowing her pride, Janne told Svein about the proposed proposal, and he replied that he must have swallowed the ring. He accepted her proposal and, borrowing a ring from one of the guests, made the engagement official. Svein, who said, "now I am 24 carats heavier" had to wait for nature to take its course, but everything worked out in the end.

Green Jelly Genes

Since jellyfish have genes that make them glow green, scientists have been tinkering with ways to use that unique phenomenon in other plants and animals. The Scottish Agricultural College in June 1999 created a potato that glowed green when it needed water. And Hertfordshire University in England announced in October 1999 that it would genetically alter Douglas spruce trees with jellyfish genes in order to create naturally illuminating Christmas trees.

Scientists were also using firefly genes in a similar process, according to research conducted in December 1999 at the University of Cincinnati. They were working on producing self-lighting Christmas trees as well as zebra fish that glowed when they detected certain pollutants in water.

Very Special Delivery

Rodney and Juanita Annis of Nictaux, Nova Scotia, a town so small that it isn't even listed in the census by Statistics Canada, have always joked that they're backwoods rednecks. So when Juanita sister sent out a Facebook message requesting addresses so she could send Christmas cards, Juanita replied with "1 tree past the squirrel's hole, 3 runs past the deer lick, 1 leap over the felled oak tree." The Christmas card, mailed from the United States, was addressed to "Hick in the Woods" at that address and, according to a January 1, 2009, article in the Canadian Press, was successfully delivered. "With Canada Post, everything's possible," a spokeswoman said. "The impossible sometimes, too."

Hit the Hershey Highway

In order to get off welfare, forty-seven-year-old Guy Masse took a job at a Zellers department store in St. Hyacinthe, Quebec, for just a couple of months in 2005. Just before Christmas, Masse discovered a number of discarded chocolate bars in the trash Dumpster and thought he would take them and give them to his children. Even though the candy bars had been thrown away, they were technically still store property and "Unfortunately, this associate breached the trust of his supervisors by removing merchandise from the store, and as a result, he was let go from his position," said Hillary Stauth, spokeswoman for Hudson's Bay Co., which owns the store chain.

A Claus Call

A stand-in Santa Claus in Conroe, Texas, found himself ho-ho-hoping he would be able to get down from a precarious position after his beard became tangled in climbing gear thirty feet off the ground. The *Conroe Courier* reported on November 19, 2007, that rock climber James Bosson, who had not practiced rappelling in costume, became snagged soon after he began his descent from the eighty-foot-tall Outlets at Conroe sign. Someone was able to toss the stranded Santa a knife, but even after he cut off the beard Bosson wasn't able to climb down and had to be rescued by the Conroe Fire Department. Battalion chief Michael Gosselin joked that the firefighters should get something extra in their stockings at Christmas after rescuing Santa Claus.

Lincoln's Emancipation

The Clintons made having a cat in the White House fashionable—but animals have found haven in the Executive Mansion for many years. One of the most interesting pets came into the Lincoln White House as a gift for Thanksgiving: Abe's admirers sent him a huge turkey. Lincoln's son Thomas ("Tad"), who was about ten years old at the time, named the bird Jack, and made him his pet. Tad was devastated when he found out Jack was going to be the guest of honor at Thanksgiving—as the main course. He threw a fit and appealed to his father to give the turkey a reprieve, at least until Christmas. President Lincoln agreed and granted a stay of execution for Jack. When Christmas rolled around, Tad again pleaded with his father for mercy. At one point he made such a commotion his father had to temporarily adjourn a cabinet meeting to see what all the screaming was about. When Honest Abe realized Tad was begging for the life of his pet, he walked back into his office, picked up a pen and piece of paper, and wrote out a document releasing Jack from his impending demise. Tad, waving the document around and screaming for joy, ran into the kitchen and showed the cook he would have to come up with another idea for Christmas dinner.

Single Santa

The October 25, 2001, *Daily News* reported that the European Union had reexamined their guidelines and determined that there was no need for Santa Claus to have a Mrs. Claus with him. EU spokesman Andrew Fielding said that giving Santa a female partner would not break down sexual stereotypes and also noted that the reindeer displayed pulling Santa's sleigh were all female. (Females reindeer keep their antlers until the spring while male reindeer shed their antlers before winter.) This makes sense, Fielding explained, because only females "would be able to drive a fat-arsed guy in a velvet suit around the world in one night and not get lost."

Replacement Parts

S hopping isn't among most men's idea of an ideal time even if they're with a female companion. The management of the Braehead Shopping Center in Glasgow, Scotland, understood the plight of the male tagalong and started providing "surrogate boyfriends" that women could hire to shop with them. On September 30, 2004, a spokeswoman for the shopping center explained the program to ABC News: "The Shopping Boyfriend is the ultimate retail therapist: enthusiastic, attentive, admiring and complimentary." The substitute significant other would even go the extra mile to make a female shopper happy: "He will browse with the girlfriend for hours on end. He'll even say her butt looks small."

Naughty or Nice

A Pfungstadt, Germany, man in his midfifties, dressed as Santa Claus at a local market, could probably expect a lump of coal and twigs for Christmas after he was accused of slapping a nine-year-old boy and locking him in a broom closet. On December 4, 2001, Reuters reported that a group of children had taunted Santa about what he was wearing under his fur-lined red suit. Police did not detain Santa and said, "He vehemently denies having done that."

Bunker Down for Christmas

Thirty-year-old Colin Wood of London, England, was so sick of the stress of dealing with his family during the Christmas holiday that he spent $430 to rent a getaway location for two weeks. That's not too strange until you find out that the location was a decommissioned bunker in Essex, complete with blast-proof doors and ten-foot-thick concrete. In a December 21, 2001, Reuters report, bunker owner Michael Parrish said, "I gather it's like being in prison without the exercise hour or worse because you can't look out of the prison bars at the sun or the moon." Wood wasn't alone in his desire to be alone; he was one of fifty people to place bids on an Internet auction site for the chance to stay in the bunker.

Wood left the bunker a week early because, as he told Reuters on December 25, 2001, "It was great but I was dying for a pint and the idea of a spending another week was too much."

Better to Give Than to Receive

Over the course of three days, a man in New York City wearing a red Santa hat passed out $25,000 in $100 bills to strangers on the street—and he had been doing it for the past twenty-two years. The anonymous giver from Kansas City, Missouri, said that he was once destitute in Mississippi when the owner of a diner gave him twenty dollars "in a way that didn't embarrass me." A Macy's security guard, James Frazier, was a recipient of the Secret Santa's generosity. "I was standing on 34th Street doing my job and a big guy came up to me and said 'Hi.' I said 'Hi,' and he gave me a $100 bill." The nineteen-year-old guard told *USA Today* on December 20, 2001, that he planned to spend the miracle money on his newly born son.

Xing Out Christmas

You would think that the Puritans, who were known for their religious fervor, must have loved Christmas . . . but they didn't. In fact, they passed a law in 1659 outlawing the celebration of Christmas. A five-shilling fine was levied against anyone "found observing, by abstinence from labor, feasting or any other way, any such days as Christmas day." They considered Christmas "an extreme forgetfulness of Christ, by giving liberty to carnal and sensual delights." For Puritans, they sure talked about sex a lot, didn't they?

The Jurors Have Reached a Decision

According to a December 20, 2005, AP story, jurors at a molestation trial in Denver, Colorado, were appalled by the man's crime against his innocent ten-year-old stepdaughter and disheartened that the trial, held in December, would mean the little girl wouldn't have a Christmas. So jury forewoman Jennifer Volk, after sentencing the man to prison for eight years to life, asked the judge if she could take up a collection from coworkers to buy presents for the little girl and her family. In order "to provide the family with a little holiday happiness," Volk raised $500. "This family was traumatized," said the detective in charge of the case. "And they went and did something about it." In an interesting twist, the name of the detective was Ken Klaus.

Petite Père Noël

S tanding at four foot two inches, six-year-old Joel Demmon of
Bellingham, Washington, was probably one of the smallest
Santa Clauses around. The third grader loved to dress up as the
Jolly Old Elf and give away hundreds of small wrapped presents
(including ones he received with fast food meals). When Demmon
wanted to spread some Christmas cheer at Bellis Fair Mall he was
told by their assistant marketing director, Cara Buckingham, that
he was "competing" with the mall's Santa and was asked to leave.
"He cried on the way out of the mall," his mother Tracey said in a
December 19, 2001, article in the *Los Angeles Times*. "He doesn't
understand why he can't give away presents."

Roasting on an Open Fire

Like a lot of people, fifty-two-year-old Blade Hannon of Medford, Oregon, liked to decorate his house for Christmas. But unlike a lot of people, Hannon took a unique approach to what Santa roasted on an open fire: not chestnuts, but the Grinch. Hannon's Father Christmas gleefully turned the handle of a rotisserie with a grimacing green Grinch cooking away. "There have been so many people stopping here that it's blocking traffic," Hannon said in a December 12, 2001, AP article. Neighbors had mixed opinions. "This thing is just gruesome," said one. "I like it," said another. "The guy who did it must be a sick puppy."

No Compete Claus

A department store in Cornwall, England, needed a Father Christmas character at the store, so it asked the Job Center in Liskeard to post an ad for the position. No dice, replied the Job Center—advertising for a "Father" Christmas would be sexual discrimination. Trago Mills owner Bruce Robinson replied that he would not discriminate, but "the person, if female, should . . . have a) a deep voice; b) whiskers; c) a big belly; and d) no readily discernible bosom." According to the November 29, 2001, *Manilla Standard*, the agency relented and placed the ad, complete with the limitation to male applicants.

The Twelve Daze of Christmas

Renee Wilson-Wicker, chorale director at Grayson High School in Georgia, made some parents cross when she took liberties with the lyrics for the traditional Christmas song "The Twelve Days of Christmas." In Wilson-Wicker's version of the song, the partridge gets blown out of the pear tree with a shotgun, the turtledoves are "strangled," and the French hens are made into French hen soup. Wilson-Wicker defended her rewriting of the song, which she penned for the school's holiday concert, by telling concerned parents that they were meant to be "lighthearted and silly." Fortunately, the administration at the school backed the Wilson-Wicker artistic decision.

Five Golden Rings

I thought discharging my gun would help me discharge my anger," said forty-seven-year-old James Craig Wilson of Vancouver, Washington. Wilson was preparing to decorate his house for Christmas when he discovered that his string of outdoor lights were horribly tangled (he claims his wife simply balled them up and threw them in the garage last year). As he tried to untangle them in his driveway, his daughter pulled in and drove over them. That's when the gunfire came into play. Wilson told his wife and daughter not to be afraid, then he went into the backyard and fired his pistol into a pile of dirt. According to a December 5, 2001, article in the *Manila Standard*, five squad cars quickly responded to the gunshots and arrested Wilson on charges of reckless endangerment.

A woman called a Walmart store before the Christmas holidays and asked, "How long is a nine-foot [artificial] Christmas tree box?" It's not a strange question, as the tree comes in several pieces, but then she added, "Because I need to know if I need to bring one car or two."

That Takes the Cake

The notorious fruitcake. It's more than just the butt of thousands of Christmastime jokes—it's also impervious to submachine gunfire and easily survives a plummet from a tall building. According to Camille Hayes, who conducted tests for the *Reno Gazette-Journal*, "The larger cake proved especially resilient [to gunfire]. Rather than shattering it into the smithereens we had expected, the volley of bullets merely nibbled at its edges." The December 24, 2001, article did offer one way to destroy the super-durable delicacy: Run over it with a one-and-a-half-ton sports utility vehicle.

Getting the Bird

In order to get the perfect Norman Rockwell Christmas dinner, one must find the perfect plump turkey. So when two women in a South Wales supermarket simultaneously spotted a flawless fowl, they both pounced—on each other. The loser of the tug-of-war didn't graciously give the victor the bird; she yelled, "I hope you burn it on Christmas Day!" To which, according to a December 24, 2001, BBC News report, the winner of the prized poultry responded by smashing the woman over the head with it. A security guard at the store claimed that the brawl was taken up again in the parking lot and that one of the women returned to the store crying and missing patches of hair.

Surprise Package

Judy Money of Council Bluffs, Iowa, received a box in the mail from her brother, and when she opened it she found a beautiful ornate box—but it was broken. So Money decided to return the box to Walmart for a refund. When she called her brother Marvin Tippery to thank him for the gift and explain what she had done, he yelled at her. "No. No, you didn't!" Tippery screamed. "Your sister was in there!" Their sister had died two weeks before Christmas and, according to a December 29, 2001, article in the *Omaha World-Herald*, the box contained a portion of her ashes. Money was horrified when she rushed back to Walmart and learned that they had already disposed of the broken box. Three days later, the broken box, along with Money's sister's ashes, were found at a local landfill and returned.

Four Calling Birds

When a 911 operator in Kalispell, Montana, received a call from a number with "a history . . . for sending ambulances" police were immediately dispatched. According to police spokesperson Mike Klem Kalispell, when police arrived on the scene the owners weren't even home. So who made the emergency call? "We assume the dog chased the cat, and somehow the phone got knocked over, and the speed dial called 911," Kalispell said. In a December 26, 2001, article in the *Daily Inter Lake*, police reported that they would not be taking the animals into custody. "It's Christmas," Kalispell said. "And we don't want the animal rights activists getting all over us on that one."

VERY YOUNG CALLER TO 911 OPERATOR:

"Do you know Santa Claus's phone number?"

Don't Be So Testy!

Several customers at the Cavendish Square mall in Cape Town, South Africa, complained about one of the plastic reindeer used in the mall's Christmas display. According to a December 12, 2002, article in the *Cape Argus*, the complaints arose because of the decorations on the only male reindeer—basically, his Christmas balls. The reindeer's hanging ornaments are "anatomically correct for an animal of that size," said the manager of Display House, the company that designed the display. And if you ever saw them you wouldn't say they glowed, but since the reindeer's hindquarters were facing the shoppers they got a good look at his reindeer games. The company dispatched Hein Conradie to "fix" the situation by removing the reindeer's charms.

Quit Toying Around

A Walmart store in Sterling, Colorado, gave permission to the Toys for Tots charity organization to place a huge box in the store's lobby to collect toys for needy children. "I've been keeping an eye on that box every time I went to Walmart, and was so excited as it slowly began to fill," said Susan Kraich, who organized the local drive. But when she came to collect the "nearly full" box, she was surprised to find that the box was completely empty. According to a December 5, 2002, article in the *Sterling Journal-Advocate*, Kraich discovered that the store's manager, Brad Barritt, had ordered his employees to put all the merchandise back on the shelves unless it was accompanied by a receipt to prove it had been purchased. This would be a case of "bah, humbug" except that Barritt, saying that Walmart is "very community minded" and that he'd "hate to see a discrepancy over a few toys change that perception in the eyes of the public" donated $425 worth of toys to the drive.

No Wonder
He's Got a Red Nose

'Santa' Steals Painkiller from Drugstore" read a December 16, 2002, article from the Associated Press. Captain Mike Spraker of the Chester, Virginia, police force said the "Santa" in question obtained an undisclosed amount of the painkiller OxyContin from the Eckerd Drugstore at gunpoint and fled on foot. Police lost the white-bearded bandit and reported that "No reindeer or sleds were observed in the area." Spraker said police "immediately contacted the North Pole and verified Santa was there." And to make sure that any children hearing the report were not confused, he emphasized that "This Santa was definitely an impostor."

Bearing Gifts

He carries a sack on his back, he's merry, and he delivers packages to people, but his name isn't Santa Claus; it's Murray Christmas, and he's a mailman. This postal carrier from Fort St. John, British Columbia, was born Murray Trondson in Flin Flon, Manitoba, but his life and his last name changed in 1995. "At a Christmas party someone said 'Merry Christmas, Murray Christmas,'" he said in a December 26, 2001, AP article. His name, his good-natured disposition, and the fact that he has sleigh bells on his mailbag have made Murray Christmas a man who not only brings letters but also smiles; however, it comes at a price. "It's a name to live up to. I have to be conscious of it because sometimes I don't feel too Christmasy."

Getting into a Pickle

Most people have heard of the Walt Disney World Christmas Day Parade, but how about Berrien Springs, Michigan's Christmas Pickle Parade? The parade has been held every year since 1992 and is led by the Grand Dillmeister. People come from all over to relish in various types of pickles, including sweet pickles, original spears, kosher dill spears, genuine dills, hamburger dills, batter-dipped fried pickles, and the festival's traditional chocolate-covered gherkins. So is the town famous for its pickles, pickling plants, or cucumber farms? Nope, just the parade. Organizers toss free pickles to spectators, Santa comes by in a llama-drawn cart, and, of course, there is a pickle prince and princess. You could say the town's parade is their bread and butter.

Reindeer Names

When "A Visit from Saint Nicholas" was first published on December 23, 1823, in the New York's *Troy Sentinel*, the author was listed as anonymous and the last two reindeer were called "Dunder" and "Blixem." The poem was reprinted for the next thirteen years without attributing it to any author. Then in 1836, a reprint of the poem listed Clement Clarke Moore, a Bible professor at New York's Theological Seminary, as the true author (although there is considerable speculation that the poem was actually written by Henry Livingston, Jr.—but that's another story).

Anyway, the next year publisher Charles Fenno Hoffman printed the poem but changed the names of the last two reindeer to "Blixen" to rhyme with "Vixen" (somewhere between 1837 and 1844 the name was again changed to "Blitzen") and "Dunder" to "Donder," perhaps keeping it in line with English pronunciation. So "Donder" remained "Donder" for about 116 years until Robert May changed it to "Donner" in a booklet for a Montgomery Ward promotional giveaway. And ten years later the name "Donner" was permanently engrained in the public's mind when May's brother-in-law Johnny Marks turned it into the song we know as "Rudolph the Red-Nosed Reindeer."

All That Glitters Is Not Gold

According to a December 16, 2002, report on ABC News, a would-be robber was arrested in Munich, Germany, after he was easily identified following a botched holdup of a lottery ticket shop. The thief threatened the store's owner with an air pistol, and the shopkeeper's wife retaliated with the closest weapon at hand—a can of Christmas glitter spray. The shiny and stunned robber quickly fled the store, leaving his wallet behind. A short time later, still covered in glitter, the thief reported his wallet as stolen to Munich police and was arrested on the spot.

Ta-Dah!

"Nora," a performing bear, was scheduled to entertain forty residents of a Hannover, Germany, retirement center during a Christmas party in 2000. The 485-pound brown bear "was only supposed to sit on a bench and eat fruit while her handler talked about the history of bears," said Klaus J., director of the home, who refused to give his full name because he faces charges of culpable manslaughter. Culpable manslaughter? That's right, because as the bear was being led into a hall she tripped over the wheelchair of a ninety-year-old woman and accidentally sat on her. According to an August 7, 2002, Reuters article, the woman couldn't bear the weight and later died from her injuries.

The Straw That Broke the Camel's Back

On December 30, 2002, police pulled over forty-three-year-old Jose Galvan and twenty-one-year-old Juan Luna and charged them with transporting 220 pounds of marijuana in the back of their pickup truck. Chicago police estimated the marijuana's worth at $700,000, and both men were charged with felony possession with intent to distribute. But further testing of the suspected marijuana proved that it wasn't the illicit drug after all—it was actually hay. According to a January 24, 2003, article in the *Chicago Tribune*, the two men were hauling away hay from a dismantled Christmas Nativity scene at Saint Wenceslaus Roman Catholic Church, where they are members. The charges were dropped, but both men, born in Mexico, were detained on immigration violations. Luna faced additional, but unrelated, charges of manufacturing and delivering a controlled substance.

Classic Claus

Twenty-eight-year-old John Deckler of Brooklyn, New York, apparently had too many eggnogs on Christmas Eve 1880 and suddenly decided to be the local Santa Claus. Although he didn't have flying reindeer, Deckler jumped out of the second-story window of his house, landed on his head, and sustained a concussion.

NEWSPAPER AD:

"Christmas sale. Handmade gifts for the hard-to-find person."

On a Bad Note

Police responded to a neighbor's 911 call about screams coming from the home of Caroline Pors in Cloverdale, British Columbia, and were on the scene within minutes. Pors met them at the door and claimed there had been no one screaming at her residence. But according to a November 28, 2003, article in the *Ottawa Citizen*, she knew what the complaint was really about. Pors's fourteen-year-old daughter, Stephanie, had been singing Christmas carols. "I know my voice is bad and I'm just assuming she has my genes," Caroline said. Police made no arrests but did write in their report that the girl was "exercising her vocal chords" and there was not "any danger, except perhaps to surrounding windows."

Pot Calling the Kettle Black

Sixty-year-old Patricia Parra, a disabled bell ringer for the Salvation Army, was collecting money in front of a store in South Tucson, Arizona, when a man grabbed her collection kettle and ran. According to a December 3, 2002, article in the *Arizona Daily Sun*, forty-year-old Edward Sanders was able to take the kettle after a short struggle and then ran across the street to make his getaway. Before he made it to the other side, however, he was struck by a 1997 Honda sedan. South Tucson police sergeant Dan Snyder said Sanders was not seriously injured, and the kettle, containing $53.97, was returned. "I think God has a poetic sense of justice," Snyder said.

Magic Carpet Ride

Christmas was quickly approaching and Chuck Cole, the manager of an apartment building in Glenwood Springs, Colorado, needed to find someone to install carpet in one of his units. He ran an ad in the local paper that read: "3 hour quickie! Extra Christmas $. Cash upon completion. Glenwood. Ready right now!"—but the editor left out the headline "Carpet layer wanted." Soon his phone was ringing off the hook. "It got pretty darn kinky! One woman said she thought she could 'help me out,'" Cole said. "I started to feel like something goofy was going on so I said, 'Are you a carpet layer?' She said, 'Well, whatever.'" Another woman called Cole and informed him that she was the right person for the "quickie," especially since her husband was at work during the day. According to a December 28, 2003, *Denver Post* article, only one man responded to the ad. The newspaper, the *Glenwood Springs Post Independent,* corrected the ad the next day, and Cole was able to get his carpet installed before the holiday.

Dash Away, Dash Away, Dash Away All

I thought the last thing I wanted to do was let Blitzen get away," said TV reporter Meghan Stapleton of KTUU in Anchorage, Alaska. "Especially two days before Christmas." Stapleton was on her usual Christmas assignment to the town of North Pole to report on the activities of Santa Claus. Before her report went live, an employee of the Santa Claus House handed her a leash with a real reindeer named "Blitzen" on the other end. Suddenly Blitzen got spooked and jumped on Stapleton, knocking her down, but she held on to the leash and was dragged several feet. Her camera crew, fast on their feet but not as fast as Blitzen, was able to catch everything on tape for the delight of Internet viewers across the world. Stapleton was quoted in a December 24, 2003, AP article saying, "You can do what you feel are impactful stories, but the biggest one is where a reindeer runs over you."

In December 2006, three years after the reindeer incident, Meghan Stapleton took a position as Alaska politician Sarah Palin's senior adviser and spokeswoman. She resigned from that post in February 2010.

Bonbons

An announcement of the perfect Christmas gift for men was heralded by its designer Reinlinde Trummer and reported in a November 13, 2002, article on Ananova. Was it a new fishing rod? A deluxe bowling ball kit? If you guessed an edible bra made completely out of chocolate, then you guessed correctly. The bras, which sell for about $158 each, are guaranteed not to "let the owners down" at the wrong moment, and they won't melt in your hand.

Keep on Tracking

S alt Lake City, Utah's municipal aviation committee voted to revoke a twenty-year-old city ordinance because it was "not in keeping with the overall tone and seriousness" of city laws, airport director Tim Campbell told the city council.

Here is the official "Santa Clause":

16.16.180 Flight Over the City Minimum Altitude:
A. General Restrictions: Except as directed by FAA air traffic control, aircraft flown over residential or business areas of the city shall comply with minimum altitude as specified in regulations promulgated by the federal aviation administration.
B. Exemption for Flying Reindeer on Christmas Eve: On Christmas Eve only, flying reindeer and any cargo they may be towing shall be exempt from the provisions of subsection A of this section. (Ord. 77-04 § 12, 2004: Ord. 92-85 § 1, 1985: prior code §§ 2-3-8, 2-3-8(e))

According to September 15, 2004, article on FoxNews.com, council members rejected Campbell's argument and reinstated the ordinance.

Have a Very Careful Christmas

In 2004, the Royal Society for the Prevention of Accidents in Britain issued an "Office Party Planner" to make employers and employees aware that "there are risks that people need to be aware of" in regards to Christmas parties. Here are some of the issued warnings:

"Dancing on desks could do them and you a lot of damage."

"Party balloons can cause severe reactions, potentially deadly, in people who are allergic to latex."

"Over 1,000 people were injured by Christmas trees in 2002, so be careful when putting them up."

"Resist the temptation to photocopy parts of your anatomy—if the copier breaks, you'll be spending Christmas with glass in some painful places."

A Shot in the Dark

The mother of an eight-year-old girl who attends Geraldine Boudreaux Elementary School in Terrytown, Louisiana, suggested that the girl bring about thirty small cups of gelatin to school to sell to earn extra Christmas money. But when a teacher in the school saw liquid dripping from the girl's backpack as she was waiting for the school bus, she hauled her into the office. According to a December 7, 2004, AP article, the girl was suspended for nine days for "intent to distribute" a "look-alike drug" on campus. Why? Because the gelatin cups looked like "Jell-O shots"—alcohol-laced gelatin. The unnamed girl had to consent to drug counseling and testing before being allowed back in school.

He Knows When
You Are Sleeping

An article in the December 2004 issue of the British medical journal *Psychiatric Bulletin*, and reported by BBC News on December 1, 2004, proposes that a child's belief in Santa Claus "encourages their moral development as they believe he knows which children are good or bad." Dr. Lynda Breen, the psychiatrist who wrote the article, says the myth "is a useful ace up a parent's sleeve." But who suffers the most when the child eventually grows out of believing in Santa? "Most of the evidence suggests that children are actually quite positive when they find out the truth and it is actually parents who mourn the loss," Breen writes.

"Why are all of your Christmas CDs not out
like they are in December?"

—OVERHEARD AT THE MUSIC SECTION OF WALMART
AROUND EASTER

Run, Santa, Run

It was called the "world's biggest gathering of Santa Clauses" when 4,250 people, all dressed as Santa Claus, participated in a charity run in Newtown, Powys, in Wales. Everything was running well until "a few" of the sprinting Santas popped into a local pub. After a few pints, the thirty or so highly spirited Father Christmases got into a street brawl that had to be broken up by police, who used tear gas and truncheons. According to a December 10, 2004, UPI article, five fully suited Kris Kringles were cuffed and hauled off to jail.

Stocks and Stockings

A wind-up Santa Claus toy outperformed eight professionals in a Canadian newspaper's annual stock-picking contest in 2000. The *Globe and Mail* reported on January 15, 2001, that the plastic red and green helicopter in which Santa was sitting was pointed at the stock of Denbury Resources, Inc., a Texas-based oil and gas company. The price of the stock soared to give a return on investment of 179.2 percent. "He sleighed it," the newspaper bragged about Santa's performance, adding, "Santa will now be given an honorable retirement, in gratitude for his services in the science of investing." For the following year, the "random stock-picker" would be "Jahe, a Sumatran orangutan."

Crazy for Christmas

Sixty-five-year-old Frederick Kaercher of Warren, Michigan, was charged with murder in the stabbing death of his daughter following an argument. Kaercher, who is frequently asked to portray Santa Claus for his town's Thanksgiving parade, was arrested following the death of thirty-one-year-old Monica Kaercher. The argument started after Kaercher accused his daughter of stealing items from his house. The fight escalated until Kaercher retrieved a kitchen knife and killed his daughter. According to a November 7, 2002, AP article, they were arguing, in part, over missing Christmas decorations.

Santi-Claus

Boys and girls in the village of Mosgiel, New Zealand, are allowed to visit Saint Nick, but they're not allowed to sit on his lap anymore. According to November 28, 2003, Agence France-Presse article, Gail Thompson, secretary of the South Island Mosgiel Business Association, said the new rule was "ridiculous" but necessary. The concern, she said, was both for the children and fear of future lawsuits. "None of us really want the risk of someone saying in 15 years' time 'When we sat on Santa's knee at market day . . .' so they are sitting on elves' chairs," she said. The specially designed chairs are placed next to Santa Claus, and it is from there that the children can express their Christmas wishes. Graham Glass, who played Santa, called the ban "bloody ridiculous."

iPod for an iPod

A judge in Mercer, Pennsylvania, ordered Mark Nichols, who stole Christmas gifts from a Florida couple's van on December 24, 1998, to sell his own stereo and weight set so he would know how it felt to do without. The nineteen-year-old from Shenango Township, about fifty-five miles northwest of Pittsburgh, was ordered by Mercer County judge Francis Fornelli to sell his $2,000 stereo and $1,800 weight set and give the money to charity. Nichols was also sentenced to two years' probation. According to a May 14, 1999, AP article, Nichols apologized to the judge for stealing and claimed he was intoxicated at the time.

A Real Christmas Surprise

Wolfgang Dircks of Bonn, Germany, had set up his bank account to automatically pay his rent each month. But in November 1998, after two or three months went by and the rent invoices stopped being paid, his landlord decided to find out what the problem was. He knocked but no one answered, so he let himself in with his passkey. He found a skeleton reclining in a chair in front of a television set (in the "on" position but no longer working). Beside him were still-twinkling Christmas lights. Next to the chair was a nearly five-year-old television program guide, dated December 5, 1993, which authorities declared to be his date of death.

A Claus for Concern

Two Swiss banks, UBS and Raiffeisenbank, have banned Santa Claus and his helpers from entering their branches. Are they being Grinches? Nope, they're afraid that people dress as "Samichlaus" ("Santa Claus" in Swiss German) and his helpers, "Schmutzli," who blacken their faces, might be robbers in disguise. According to a December 1, 1999, article in the *Orlando Sentinel*, the banks warned their employees to be on the lookout for fat, bearded men who go by various names: Santa Claus or Saint Nick in England and America, Sinterklaas in the Netherlands and Belgium, Sankt Nikolaus in Germany, and Saint Nicolas in France.

Well, It Rhymes

Attorney Richard Ganulin filed a lawsuit in Cincinnati, Ohio, challenging Congress's authority to make Christmas a federal holiday in violation of the concept of the separation of church and state. But according to a December 7, 1999, AP article, U.S. district judge Susan J. Dlott threw out the lawsuit and began her twenty-four-page ruling with some lyrical legalese. Her nine-stanza poem goes, in part:

> *The court will address*
> *Plaintiff's seasonal confusion*
> *Erroneously believing Christmas*
> *MERELY a religious intrusion.*

> *We are all better for Santa,*
> *the Easter Bunny too,*
> *and maybe the Great Pumpkin,*
> *to name just a few!*

> *An extra day off*
> *is hardly high treason;*
> *it may be spent as you wish,*
> *regardless of reason.*

> *One is never jailed,*
> *for not having a tree,*
> *for not going to church,*
> *for not spreading glee!*

> *The court will uphold,*
> *seemingly contradictory causes,*
> *decreeing "The Establishment"*
> *and "Santa"*
> *both worthwhile claus(es).*

Ganulin had planned an appeal.

Artificial Tree—
Real Problem

To quell the complaints and concerns of people who feared that a live Christmas tree could pose a fire hazard, state officials in Jackson, Mississippi, installed an artificial tree in the capitol and ornately decorated its silk branches—and it promptly caught on fire. The capitol was quickly filled with smoke, and about seventy-five capitol workers, legislators, and reporters had to be evacuated for several hours. According to a December 13, 1999, article in the *Clarion Ledger*, there were no injuries or serious damage. Fire officials pointed to electrical problems with lights at the base of the tree as the cause of the blaze.

Don't Do the Crime If You Can't Do the Rhyme

Before Christmas 2007, police in Middlesbrough, in northeast England, sent out Christmas cards—to would-be burglars. Detective Inspector Chris Sadler said the cards were part of the ongoing Operation Castle—a crackdown on house burglaries in his town.

> If you're tempted into crime,
> expect to do some festive time.
> Instead of singing "Jingle Bells,"
> you'll spend Christmas in a cell.
>
> Stick to the rules of Operation Castle,
> if you want to avoid this yuletide hassle.
>
> Thinking of you at Christmas,
> from all at the Operation Castle team.

Sadler said the cards were meant to be "tongue-in-cheek, but the message is very serious." He explained, "If you commit crime and burgle people's houses over Christmas we will try to ensure you spend your Christmas inside the cells. We will be here all over Christmas. We would like a quiet time of it, but if we have to go and lock them up on Christmas morning we will do it."

Running A-Monk

To refortify his soul, fifty-eight-year-old Ray John was supposed to spend a peaceful and alcohol-free Christmas on Caldey Island, off the west coast of Wales, in the sanctuary of nineteen Cistercian monks. But John smuggled in his own supply of liquor and started singing Christmas carols loudly at midnight. The monks, who have taken a vow of silence for twelve hours per day, weren't able to say anything to John—they couldn't even "hush" him. "He was up all night making a terrible racket. We observe a vow of silence but it wasn't a very silent night—even if it was Christmas," said Abbot Father Daniel Van Santvoort. "I'm afraid some of us had very little peace that night. All we could do was lie in our beds and cover our ears." According to a January 13, 2000, BBC News piece, John was asked to leave the island the next day, which he did, but he didn't stop drinking. Police found him unconscious on a railway line, and he was fined eighty dollars for drunk and disorderly conduct.

A Dance to Remember

Malberry Smith, Jr., of Savannah, Georgia, never paid the $5 fee for renting the ballroom where his senior class held its Christmas dance. "I never got a bill for it and I guess I just kind of forgot it," said Smith. This doesn't sound like a big deal until you realize that the dance was held on December 18, 1931, sixty-nine years before Smith decided to pay the tab. "I've been settling out some affairs, and I figured I'd better do something before it got too late," said Smith, who cut a check for the $5 fee plus $513.50 in interest. He calculated the interest at 7 percent from the dance's date to July 1, 2000. Smith's check came as "a total surprise" and went to help pay for restoration work on the 1924 building in Atlanta. "It was not a gift, it was the satisfaction of a debt," Smith, a prominent lawyer, said. "I'm just glad I was in a position to make it right after all these years."

A White Christmas

In December 2000, military police in Jacarepaguá, Brazil, thought a street vendor selling Santa Claus dolls was acting suspicious, and when he took off running they knew something wasn't right. They caught the unidentified man and then took a closer look at the dolls he was selling: They were all stuffed with cocaine. Police confiscated more than two hundred grams of cocaine and arrested the vendor for drug trafficking.

"Father Christmas Was Punched in His Grotto"
—*Dorset (England) Echo* HEADLINE, DECEMBER 2, 2008

A Real Gas!

A tear gas canister accidentally tossed into a city building claimed seven hundred unintended casualties. Fortunately, they weren't people. They were stuffed animals donated to the Clarksville, Tennessee, Fire Department to give to needy kids at Christmas. The police were doing "practice maneuvers," and were supposed to use a look-alike canister that held benign gas but instead used real tear gas, which settled on the stuffed animals like dust. Attempts to clean the stuffed animals failed. According to a December 3, 2000, article in the *Tuscaloosa News*, police worked with local retailers to help replace the damaged animals.

A Judicial Tie

British magistrate Hector Graham was at the most dramatic part of the trial in Luton, Bedfordshire, in England. He was about to pass sentence, and the entire courtroom was silent. "He had got to the part about how serious an offense it was when all of a sudden 'Santa Claus Is Coming to Town' started up," a court spokesman said. Was it an obnoxious ring tone of a spectator's cell phone? Nope, according to a December 22, 2000, article in the *Independent*, it was Graham's musical Christmas tie that he had received from his wife as a gift. "He didn't have a clue how to stop it and was extremely embarrassed, especially because after that, it went into two more Christmassy songs and finished with 'We Wish You a Merry Christmas.'"

A Christmas Eve Blast

A twenty-two-year-old man died on Christmas Eve 2000 when he and a friend were playing William Tell with a .25-caliber semiautomatic pistol. Aurora, Illinois, police were looking for Adrian Lorenzo Quintana-Galindo in connection with the shooting death of his friend Manuel Dominguez-Quintero. Apparently, Quintana-Galindo had Dominguez-Quintero place a plastic cup on his head and attempted to shoot it off but instead hit Dominguez-Quintero in the forehead, killing him instantly. Investigators were still trying to calculate the distance between the two men with the shooting occurred.

No Twigs or Coal
for Santa

According to a December 23, 1999, article in the Chilean newspaper *Las Últimas Noticias*, a twenty-eight-year-old man dressed as Santa Claus was riding in a truck on the way to the town of Tocopilla to distribute candy. A group of children began following his truck and demanding he toss them some candy, as well. When he didn't, they began pelting him with stones. He became disoriented and a few of the children boarded the truck and stole candy and toys from his sack. "They left me full of goose eggs," he said. The three-hundred-pound Santa was left bloodied and bruised. To make matters worse, he realized that the glue he had used to affix his beard had burned his face.

You Could Even Say It Glows

People have constructed Santa's Grotto, those large cavern-like areas that lead to Santa, out of different kinds of material for decades, but only one, so far, has been made out of disused nuclear waste containers. Apprentices from the Dounreay, Scotland, nuclear power station built their grotto in late December 1999. Hundreds of children passed through it to visit Santa before the manufacturing material was identified. The UK Atomic Energy Authority, which runs the plant, promised that the containers had been decontaminated, were completely safe, and had been used only to store low-level nuclear materials, such as discarded clothes and towels from workers who dealt with nuclear waste. "We have very rigorous procedures for cleaning up and decontamination. Use of these materials is quite normal, but we can see how parents are sensitive when their children are involved," Beth Taylor, head of corporate communications, told Reuters.

Bending the Amendment

In any debate over prayer in school, Nativity scenes and Christmas trees on state property, or statues of the Ten Commandments in courthouses, the so-called wall of separation between church and state as outlined in the Constitution is bound to be brought up. This is an interesting argument, because there is no "wall of separation between church and state" mentioned anywhere in the Constitution or the Bill of Rights. The First Amendment states only, "Congress shall make no law respecting an establishment of religion, or prohibiting the free exercise thereof." The Founding Fathers included this amendment because they didn't want the United States of America to establish a national church (like the Church of England—one of the reasons colonists broke ties with England in the first place). It seems bizarre that the Founding Fathers took the time to write everything down—but no one, not even the courts, takes the time to read it.

Be Good for Goodness' Sake

A December 7, 1999, article in the *Semanario*, the organ for the Catholic Church in Guadalajara, Mexico, referred to Santa Claus "as a fat clown, with the chapped cheeks of a heavy beer drinker, the big stomach of a bon vivant, the nose of a drunk" and the "boots of a gendarme." The article argued that Saint Nicholas, from whom Santa Claus evolved, was a generous man of wealth who practiced anonymous acts of charity and later became a miracle-working bishop in Myra (in modern-day Turkey) and the protector of orphans, widows, and sailors. "What happened to the bishop?" the article entitled "Santa Claus, the Usurper," asked. "What happened to his miter . . . his sacred vestments and his consecrated hands blessing the devoted?" It continued by stating that Santa Claus has "usurped the name and the personality of Saint Nicholas. Let's not permit him to usurp the place of Christ."

Ham Hock or Hock the Ham

A truck containing hundreds of turkeys and hams was hijacked by robbers in Brazil's Minas Gerais as it was heading for the town of Itaperuna in neighboring state of Rio de Janeiro. The misappropriated meat was meant to fill the Christmas food baskets of five hundred Brazilian police officers. The baskets, which all military police in the state receive, also included mayonnaise, oil, olives, a bottle of local sparkling wine, raisins, stewed peaches, and sardines. But before you could break a wishbone, the owner of the meat company whose truck was robbed sent more turkeys the next day. The 2000 Reuters article reported that the thieves were still at large.

According to a July 22, 2003, article in the *Charleston Daily Mail*, an unidentified thirty-year-old man was sentenced to probation for entering a living Nativity scene located in front of a funeral home the previous Christmas and having sex with one of the sheep.

Checking It Twice

During a routine review of unclaimed state funds in Boston, Massachusetts, the state treasurer's office discovered a check for $1,112.50 made out to Santa Claus. State law requires that all unclaimed checks be turned over to the treasurer's office, whose responsibility it is to locate the intended recipients. In a December 18, 2000, AP article, treasury spokesman Dwight Robson said, "We have no idea who this property belongs to. . . . Perhaps," Robson speculated, "it was a check or money order for some kind of Christmas fund."

Just Another Day

Ninette Smith, a switchboard operator for the Sheraton Chicago Hotel and Towers, complained to the Chicago office of the Equal Employment Opportunity Commission because the hotel required all switchboard operators to greet callers with "Happy Holidays" from Thanksgiving until New Year's Day. The EEOC sued the hotel claiming that this was a violation of Smith's religious freedom. "'Happy holidays' is generally considered a generic term in our business," said Ellen Butler, spokeswoman for the hotel. "We use it because it doesn't mention any holidays specifically by name." To try and accommodate Smith, hotel management suggested an alternative salutation. "We told her she could just say, 'Greetings,'" said Butler. The EEOC said in November 1993 that that wasn't good enough and that they were still going ahead with the lawsuit because, "They only wanted her to say it during the Christmas season, so it is a violation."

How About Festivus, Then?

Concord, New Hampshire, junior high school student Tiffany Tropp asked a group of her classmates who were singing Christmas songs to stop. Troop, who is Jewish, complained to the principal shortly before Christmas break in 1993, saying that the holiday songs made her feel uncomfortable. She explained that when she asked the students to quit singing they began to tease her and that one classmate told her that Christmas is about "peace and love" and then shoved her into a locker.

Can't We Just Get Along?

Henry County High School, in Paris, Tennessee, was forced to cancel its 1994 Christmas concert after the chorus teacher allegedly bashed the band director in the face with a chair. Kenneth Humphrey, who is both a county commissioner and a minister, was charged with aggravated assault against Martin Paschall. Police reports stated that Humphrey and Paschall had gotten into an argument over which one of them would make an announcement at the concert.

Deal or No Deal

A loyalist spy had learned that George Washington and his small Continental army had secretly crossed the Delaware River earlier on the day after Christmas, 1776, and were headed toward Trenton, New Jersey. The spy arrived at the home of merchant Abraham Hunt where the leader of the Hessian army, Colonel Johann Rall, was drinking and playing cards. The colonel refused to break from his game of cards and demanded the spy hand over the written message, which he promptly put in his vest pocket without reading. Colonel Rall was awakened the next day to the sound of musket fire and, having no time to organize or rally his troops, suffered a crushing defeat at the hands of Washington's army— their first over the British. He also sustained two wounds that lead to his death the following day.

Politics as Usual

O n this day, when we celebrate the birth of a homeless child who later became the Prince of Peace . . . " began Hillary Clinton's official holiday greeting at a December 22, 1997, press conference with housing secretary Andrew Cuomo. Vice President Gore commented, "Speaking from my own religious tradition in this Christmas season, two thousand years ago a homeless woman gave birth to a homeless child in a manger because the inn was full." Actually, Mary and Joseph weren't homeless. The only reason they sought refuge in a Bethlehem stable was because they were traveling. Remember the story? The Roman emperor Augustus wanted to have a list of all the people in the empire, to make sure they paid their taxes, so he ordered everyone to return to the town where their families originally came from and enter their names in a census.

Oh, Oh, Oh, Christmas Tree!

You don't really know which ones have been sprayed. You're gambling, and you won't really know until you get it inside," said Washington State University groundskeeper Kappy Brun. A December 8, 1998, AP article told how the Pullman, Washington, groundskeeper and municipal park workers were taking revenge on thieves looking for free Christmas trees. They smeared a rancid mix of oil, water, essence of skunk, and coyote urine on the bark of various trees. The mixture froze on the trunks and had no noticeable smell—until the tree was warmed up in somebody's house.

Can't See the Forest for the Trees

Traditions, like most things, start off small, and over time they grow and grow. Well, that's just what happened when, to show their Christmas spirit, students of Madison East High School in Madison, Wisconsin, brought in three hundred Christmas trees to school. The principal felt forced to enact a tree ban during the 1998 Christmas season, which students took as an affront to their holiday tradition. "It's bogus," said Matt Mellenthin, a senior. "It's just for fun and it's only a tradition." But school district spokesman Mike McCabe defended the principal's deforestation efforts, saying, "They create a little forest there. The fire marshal went as far as to threaten the school with a fine."

Fanatic Santa

Chip Crabtree and his wife, Lori, took their sons (ages two, four, and six) to visit Santa at their local Jacksonville, Florida, mall. But when Santa saw Lori wearing a Gators sweatshirt, he remarked, "Santa Claus doesn't like Gator fans. . . . Santa Claus wishes that Florida State would beat the Gators in the Sugar Bowl." Soon Santa and the Crabtrees were exchanging unpleasant remarks, and Santa stormed off the stage and left the mall. According to a 1999 account, Crabtree explained to his confused children that he wasn't the real Santa. "Sometimes Santa uses helpers, and this one was an impostor," he said. Crabtree's six-year-old said he knew it wasn't Santa, because "there wasn't any magic in his eyes."

Deer, Deer, Deer

The National Park Service removed nine deer from the Pageant of Peace on the Washington Mall's Ellipse behind the White House because of pressure from People for the Ethical Treatment of Animals. Traditionally, each Christmas, the deer have been allowed to graze in a twenty-by-thirty-foot pen, symbolizing Santa's reindeer. But one animal rights activist told the *Washington Post* in 1998 that the deer looked "sad."

According to a
December 11, 2001, Reuters
article, the United Self-Defense
Forces, a notorious right-wing
death squad in Colombia,
sent e-mail Christmas cards
to their soldiers across the
countryside, wishing
them "peace."

Two-Hit Wonder

Mark Calvert, like a lot of people, has two jobs. One of his jobs is at Liquidation World in Seattle, Washington, where he dresses as Santa Claus and greets shoppers as they look for bargains. His other job is as the host of *Bong Hit Championship*, a public-access show whose theme has Calvert using a stopwatch to time how long someone can hold in a hit from a marijuana water pipe. A patron of Liquidation World came across Calvert's show and watched as Calvert cheered on a fourteen-year-old caller as he took a major bong hit. She said she was appalled to hear Calvert refer to himself as a "a bona fide Santa," and give the name and location of the store. In a December 8, 1998, AP article, a spokesman for Liquidation World said the manager was unaware of Calvert's other line of work before he was hired. I'm sure Calvert was soon liquidated from Liquidation World.

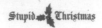

The Great Santa Race

DeWayne Lofton, a black man who wanted to portray Santa Claus at the Barton Creek Square mall in Austin, Texas, filed a lawsuit charging racial discrimination when he was denied the job. According to a December 11, 1998, AP article, Lofton was told by Santa Plus, a St. Louis–based company that contracts with retailers to fill Santa positions, that the mall didn't hire black Santa Claus. A Santa Plus manager told him, "When I spoke to you over the phone, I did not realize that you were black. I'll have to check with the mall to see if it would be OK to hire, you know." The mall denied this claim and said they don't have any such discriminatory policy in place. Lofton was seeking unspecified damages from both the mall and Santa Plus.

Kris Krumble

Flight Sergeant Nigel Rogoff of the Royal Air Force Sport Parachute Association was hired to dress as Santa Claus and parachute onto a soccer field in front of forty thousand screaming fans. During the halftime show between Aston Villa and Arsenal in Birmingham, England, Santa slowly descended toward the field when suddenly, "He banged on the stand and then fell to the ground," said witness Peter Hargraves, who attended the soccer match. "No one could believe it." According to a December 16, 1998, AP article, Rogoff, who was a veteran of more than six thousand parachute jumps, suffered two broken legs, a fractured pelvis, and broken ribs and—what's worse for the soccer fans—delayed the second half by fifteen minutes.

A Slice of Good Cheer

A fifty-five-year-old woman from Oostzaan, in the Netherlands, must have really wanted a silent night: She stabbed her husband in the chest because he wouldn't stop singing "Silent Night." She claimed she couldn't stand her husband's singing anymore and that he had repeated the same song for more than five hours before she cut his solo career short. A December 28, 1998, Reuters article reported that the man was transported to a local hospital and was expected to make a full recovery. The woman was arrested and her fate was at the mercy of the public prosecutor.

A Long-Shot Gift

Thirteen-year-old Ricardo Soto of Fort Hancock, Texas, wanted a Nintendo game so badly for Christmas that, when he didn't get one, he hid in the brush alongside Interstate 10 on Christmas Day and shot at a tractor-trailer truck he believed was transporting video games. His nine-year-old brother, David Soto, told the Associated Press on December 27, 1995, that Ricardo told him he wanted to "shoot a trailer and get Nintendos out of it." He shot the rig twice, and when he fired his .22-caliber rifle again he accidentally shot Alberto Tarango, who was driving with his wife in their pickup truck. "I guess he thinks every truck had toys," said county sheriff Arcadio Ramirez. Soto was charged with deadly conduct in juvenile court.

Nun-Sense

The nuns of Saint Cecilia's congregation in Nashville, Tennessee, asked their maintenance men to pick up a Christmas tree that was donated to their order. They returned later that day with the tree, but it was the wrong tree. When the tree's donor called and asked why the tree hadn't been picked up from his front porch the nuns asked the maintenance men where they got the tree, but they couldn't remember. The embarrassed nuns turned for help to the *Tennessean* newspaper, which printed a plea for the owner of the tree to contact the nuns. When they finally discovered whose tree they had inadvertently stolen, the men returned it immediately. The tree's gracious owner, who said she never thought she'd see the tree again, rewarded the men with a plate of cookies. "We're glad there's a happy ending to the story," said Saint Cecilia's Stephanie Sundock in a December 22, 1997, AP article.

I'll Drink to That

Cosmo Zinkow, a thirteen-year-old eighth grader in Griffin Middle School in Smyrna, Georgia, wanted to get his teacher something special for Christmas. He decided a simple apple wasn't enough but figured a fine wine that goes good with fruit would do the trick. He brought in a gift-wrapped bottle of Mouton Cadet Bordeaux wine and presented it to his French teacher. The teacher, who doesn't drink, reported the child and his gift as a violation of Georgia laws against possession of alcohol by a minor and bringing alcohol onto school property. "When you take a Christmas gift to the teacher, wrapped and in a box with a bow and a card, that's not possessing alcohol," Cosmo's father, Bill Zinkow, told the *Atlanta Journal-Constitution* newspaper on December 21, 1997. "I felt like this was an appropriate gift for her," Zinkow said. The boy has an A average in course work but was suspended from school for ten days. He was allowed to make up tests he missed during his suspension.

It's in the Mail

Robert and Dorothy King of Burnaby, British Columbia, were curious why they had never heard from their friends, the Bryces, who had moved to Hamilton. The Kings were expecting the Bryces to send a note giving them their new address, but they never received anything and thought they had just forgotten about them. But in April 1998 the Kings received a Christmas card from their old friends. "They said Merry Christmas to us and said the kids are OK," said ninety-year-old Robert King. But by the time they received the card, the "kids" were twenty-two years older than when the card was sent. "It just showed up in the mail with an eight-cent stamp on it," said Robert, and noted that the postmark was December 16, 1976. King said he and his wife will now try to contact their old neighbors but complained to Canada Post about the twenty-two-year delay in delivering their mail. "It doesn't happen very often, but when it does we like to find out the circumstances," said Canada Post communications director Bob Taylor. "It possibly fell behind a vent and when we did renovations, we found it."

Reach Out and Touch Someone

Rachel Murray, from Hendon, North London, wanted to surprise her flatmate, Tony Dangerfield, with a cell phone for Christmas. So she wrapped the gift and placed it under the tree, but when Christmas came the present was nowhere to be found. She found some torn Christmas paper but no phone. After frantically searching the flat she called the phone company to retrieve the phone number and then called it. According to a 1997 Reuters article she heard the phone ringing from inside Dangerfield's bloodhound, Charlie. The dog had eaten the cell phone. They took the dog to the veterinarian who suggested they let nature take its course. Twenty-four hours later the phone made its long-distance trip through Charlie and emerged in perfect working order. No word on whether the dog enjoyed the vibrate feature or not.

Spruce Sprint

The following story comes from the "Police Reports" column of the *Glen Ellyn (IL) Press* from December 19, 1992. According to the records, twenty-one-year-old Eric Hoyt and twenty-five-year-old Peter A. Thordason were arrested and charged with stealing Christmas trees from a lot outside a Glen Ellyn grocery store. The two denied the charges and "Thordason allegedly told police he wanted to see how long it would take him to run around the building carrying the tree while Hoyt timed him."

Agence France-Presse reported on December 26, 2003, that approximately fifty inmates at a Belas, Portugal, prison boycotted their special Christmas lunches because the bread wasn't fresh: As bakeries close on Christmas, the bread had been baked the day before.

The Donor Party

According to Queensland, Australia's *Sunday Mail*, a former employee of the municipal morgue in Brisbane, Australia, told reporters on July 10, 1994, that the morgue where he used to work routinely sold organs from corpses without their families' permission. The unnamed employee said they sold the black-market organs primarily to researchers, but in one case sold pituitary glands, collected during the late 1980s, for roughly fifty cents apiece in order to raise money to fund a staff Christmas party in 1993.

Pine-Sol Boy

S ixteen-year-old Tracy McIntyre of Stockton, California, had
suffered with notorious halitosis for several years but was never
able to find the cause of his bad breath. A December 16, 1995,
Albuquerque Journal article reported that surgeon Isam Felahy
finally discovered the problem when he removed an inch-long
tree sprig from McIntyre's right lung. Apparently, McIntyre had
accidentally inhaled the small sprig from the family Christmas tree
in 1980. When Dr. Felahy removed it, the twig was still green.

Father Christmas

Daddy is Santa!" cried one-year-old Justin Ramirez as he was about to crawl on Santa's lap at the Gallery at Metrotech in downtown Brooklyn, New York. The boy's mother, LaToya Ramriez, looked beyond the white beard and realized that the boy was right—it was her deadbeat husband, Neil Ramirez. Before Santa could reach into his bag of toys, LaToya reached into her purse and produced the family court papers she happened to have been carrying. When they arrived home, Justin insisted that what he had seen was true—his father was the real Santa Claus. "I said, 'No, Santa Claus is somebody else; Santa Claus is not daddy,'" LaToya said. "My son said: 'Yes, he is! Yes, he is! Yes, he is!'" According to a December 21, 1997, article in the *New York Daily News*, after the incident, the file for Docket No. F-05703/97 now included an Affidavit of Service: "Description of person served: 'He had on a red and white Santa Claus suit.'"

Another Class Claus

On Christmas Eve 1911, Frank J. Dotzler, a 375-pound Manhattan, New York, Republican alderman (and alternate delegate to the 1908 and 1912 Republican National Conventions) got stuck on a ladder inside a chimney while playing Santa Claus for the local children. Dotzler, a member of the East Side Fat Man's Club, was finally extricated when firemen demolished the chimney. Undaunted, Dotzler and two thinner members of his club, 240-pound Phil Fecher and 235-pound Martin Max, commandeered a peddler's cart and distributed the candy.

Christmas List

This time, the police should have checked their list twice—
because this Santa was definitely naughty and not nice.
Tracy Burnett, who was playing Santa Claus at the Rio Mall in
Wildwood, New Jersey, was arrested after a security guard caught
him shoplifting. After the police ran a background check, they
discovered that he was a wanted jolly old elf. The check showed
that Burnett had a string of prior convictions including outstanding
warrants for burglary, forgery, theft, shoplifting, and thousands
of dollars in unpaid traffic tickets. "His rap sheet is about as long
as Santa's wish list," detective Jack Kirwin said. According to a
December 18, 1997, article in the *Boca Raton News*, Burnett, who
had been serving a four-year prison term for burglary before being
paroled earlier that year, was being held without bond.

Christmas Crackers

A young girl ran up to Alan Turner, who was dressed as Santa Claus at the CanWest Mall in Victoria, British Columbia, and demanded candy from the jolly old elf. When Turner told her to ho, ho, hold on and wait, the little girl kicked him in the groin, pulled off his glasses, and pulled his beard down to his waist. After the incident, Turner was fired from his position, but he was soon hired to portray Santa at the nearby Colwood Plaza because they felt he was treated unfairly. According to a January 5, 1998, article in the *Alberta Report*, when a camera crew went to interview Turner, he grabbed his crotch, in a joking manner, to demonstrate his reaction to his previous run-in with the little girl. After the station repeatedly ran the tape of Turner's dance of the Nutcracker Suite, the Colwood Plaza fired him.

Canvasing History

Close your eyes and imagine (well, read this sentence first and then close your eyes and imagine) one of the most famous paintings of American history: *Washington Crossing the Delaware.* It's one of the most recognizable paintings and one that still stirs the blood of any patriotic American. Brave General Washington, standing in the boat, leading his men across the river on Christmas Eve, 1776, to surprise the British at the Battle of Trenton. It has all the elements of a true painting of Americana: George Washington, Christmas, and weary soldiers. What it didn't have were its facts straight. A German artist named Emanuel Leutze painted the work seventy-five years after the battle; he used American tourists as models and the Rhine River for the Delaware. He got the style of the boat wrong, the clothing was incorrect, even the American flag was wrong (the flag depicted hadn't been created at the time of the battle). But why let facts get in the way of a little history, right? And hey, it's still a nice painting.

Survey Says . . .

A survey of 904 registered voters found that 39 percent believed that Santa, known for his reputation as a public benefactor, would register as a Democrat, 22 percent considered him a Republican, and 23 were undecided. The same opinion poll, conducted between December 9 and 11, 1997, and reported by FOX News, revealed that 29 percent thought the Grinch, a Dr. Seuss creation, would be a registered Democrat while 35 percent pegged him as a Republican.

In 1901, a thief robbed a post train
in New Orleans and stole 12,568
Christmas cards.

It Was a Wonderful Life

At 1:30 A.M., a car hit a deer, crushing the grille and breaking both headlights, forcing it to stop on the side of the road. There was a delay of nine minutes before an emergency dispatcher, who received a distress call, dispatched a member of the Colorado State Patrol to investigate the accident. A few minutes after the dispatch call, another car, not seeing the vehicle, smashed into it and rolled it, killing the driver and critically wounding the passenger. The Pueblo-based dispatchers are under investigation because of the December 2009 delay. According to Colonel James Wolfinbarger, chief of the Colorado State Patrol, at least one dispatcher was "distracted," because they were "watching a Christmas movie" in the station.

Like a Bowl Full of Low-Carb Jelly

The health craze hit London in the late '90s to such an extent that local stores had a difficult time finding fat elderly men to play Santa in their Christmas grottos, according to a 1998 Reuters article. "We just cannot find any suitable actors who are still, shall we say, on the porky side. All the applicants seem to live on salads and look after their bodies," a spokesman for the Ministry of Fun, an entertainment agency, said. "They're too thin. You cannot just strap a cushion on them and hope to fool the kids because they'll suss it out straightaway," he added. The agency sent out a plea for fat actors to come forward after demand for Santas from stores and shopping malls outstripped supply.

Look Whose Mumming to Town

Mumming" is the word. But what does it mean? According to an October 2007 academic journal article by University of Missouri-Columbia researchers, it is a ritual, performed for centuries, in small fishing villages in northern Newfoundland. People disguise themselves and then stalk through the town, knocking at the doors of their neighbors and attempting to scare them. The job of the neighbor is not to be afraid and to try to guess the identity of their uninvited guest. "Mumming" occurs only during Christmastime, and the ritual is supposed to induce trust by both parties: The visitor doesn't act on his threat of violence and the host shows trust by his courage and passivity. The odd Christmas tradition is still practiced today but only on a "small scale."

Outlaw Frosty

The Powers family of Anchorage, Alaska, had a family tradition of building what they call "Snowzilla" in their front yard since 2005. The imposing sixteen-foot snowman had been a media sensation and tourist attraction since its inception and was a labor of love for Billy Powers, his family, and dozens of friends and neighbors. But in 2008, Anchorage city code enforcers left a cease-and-desist sign at the base of what would have been that year's Snowzilla, deeming that the snowman was a safety hazard. According to a December 22, 2008, article in the *Anchorage Daily News*, the declaration of Snowzilla as a public nuisance and safety hazard had nothing to do with previous accidents; it came after neighbors complained about the throngs of people the snow statue attracted every year.

❄ ❄ ❄

Two days later, the *Anchorage Daily News* reported that Snowzilla had magically appeared in the family's front yard, complete with hat and carrot nose. Billy Powers claims innocence and said he had no idea who built the twenty-five-foot snowman. In an apparent demonstration of snow rebels turning up their carrot noses to authority, a smaller version of Snowzilla was also built in front of city hall.

Santa, Eh?

Most of us believe that Santa Claus comes from the North Pole, but according to a December 24, 2008, Canwest News Service article, Santa Claus has been declared a citizen of Canada with fully authorized reentry rights. In a formal statement in Ottawa, Jason Kenney, the minister of Citizenship, Immigration, and Multiculturalism, legally made Kris Kringle a Canadian citizen. "The Government of Canada wishes Santa the very best in his Christmas Eve duties and wants to let him know that, as a Canadian citizen, he has the automatic right to reenter Canada once his trip around the world is complete," Kenney's statement said. The statement pointed out that it's obvious that Santa is a product of Canada because his traditional attire features the same colors—red and white—used in the Canadian flag.

His Bark Is Worse Than His Bite

John Christian Bradley of West St. Paul, Minnesota, was arrested for being a Christmastime Robin Hood. He allegedly stole Christmas trees from an outdoor lot and distributed them in area yards. "He was in the holiday giving mood but didn't want to pay for them," West St. Paul police lieutenant Brian Sturgeon said. When police first spotted Bradley dragging a tree down the street they didn't think much about it until a tree lot attendant reported the theft. The thirty-six-year-old fir-filching felon was arrested in connection with seven other tree-related pine-nappings. "He said he was going to give everybody a Christmas tree and that no one can sell Christmas," Sturgeon said in a December 24, 2008, article in the *St. Paul Pioneer Press*. Sturgeon also confirmed that a breath test administered when Bradley was arrested indicated he had been drinking.

A Stubborn Situation

The Three Wise Men are going to have to ride donkeys because the price of camels isn't a wise economic choice in Milwaukee, Wisconsin, anymore. For those wanting to stage live, realistic Christmas pageant Nativity scenes, it may cost $2,100 to rent three camels on Christmas Eve but only $250 for six donkeys and sheep, the *Milwaukee Journal-Sentinel* reported on December 7, 2008. "It goes up and down with the economy," Kathy Meyer, whose family owns Jo-Don Farms in Franksville, Wisconsin, told the newspaper. Camels cost so much because they have to have a handler and liability insurance—the "hump-back animals can be ornery." Also, it's supply and demand, according to Mark D. Schultz, who rents five camels out of this Glacier Ridge Animal Farm, as there are only thirty to forty camels in the whole state of Wisconsin. At the time, Schultz had rented out four of his camels and still had one ready for day work, but the fifth camel "doesn't play well with others," he said.

Pining for Justice

In 2008 an anonymous tipster alerted police to some illegal activity at Maryland's North Bethesda United Methodist Church. Was it a fixed Bingo game? A covert cake sale? No, it was the fact that the church was selling Christmas trees before December 5. A little-know law makes it illegal to sell Christmas trees prior to that date and the county inspectors had swooped in and shut the sale down. They did show some Christmas spirit, because they didn't levy Pastor Debbie Scott the proposed $500 fine. The church had held its Christmas tree sale for the previous six years without a hitch, sending the proceeds to a medical clinic in Tanzania. According to a November 28, 2009, *Washington Post* article, Pastor Scott joined the ranks of the divine underworld when she, in direct violation of the county codes, started selling Christmas trees again. It was recently uncovered that the church might also be in violation of another little-known state law that prohibits the display of Christmas trees in commercial establishments for more than twenty-one days.

Deck the Halls

Police in Westminster, California, responded to a disturbance call at the home of forty-eight-year-old Vuong Pham and soon had the situation in hand. During their visit they noticed an overabundance of outdoor Christmas decorations that had taken over Pham's Orange County home. There were dozens of wicker reindeer, several Christmas trees, plastic snowmen, inflatable Santa Claus figures, and thousands of lights. "This guy had something in every room," officer Cameron Knauerhaze said. One officer recalled a briefing about a recent rash of outdoor Christmas decoration thefts in the area and realized they had found the man who had tried to steal Christmas. "We don't understand why someone would do this," Knauerhaze told the Associated Press on December 16, 2008. "We're trying to talk to the guy, to find out if he's got other issues going on in his life, but for now, it is what it is." Police needed three trucks to haul all the Christmas contraband to the police station.

Santa Left Her Flat

Most of us have heard the obnoxious Christmas tune "Grandma Got Run Over by a Reindeer" at least once (and once is too many), but for one unidentified Palmerston, Ontario, woman the song became a reality. According to a December 8, 2009, article in the *Toronto Sun*, a forty-five-year-old woman wanting to join her friends on the Santa Claus parade float tried to jump on board without the driver's knowledge. She lost her grip and fell under the float's wheels. Her legs and torso were run over, but her injuries were not life threatening.

Pull My Beard

He's called the "Santa to the Stars." Brady White, a professional Santa who appears at Macy's in New York and makes special appearances at the homes of such celebrities as Pamela Anderson, Rene Russo, Kirstie Alley, and others has taken out an insurance policy on his beard. "All sorts of things can happen to Santa's beard and I wanted to know that it was protected. Children can be a little rough so it gets tugged and pulled a lot, and then there is the soot and the danger of being singed when I head down the chimneys," White said. Lloyd's of London reported on their Web site on December 20, 2006, that White has taken out a policy on his "natural growth white beard [which] is a valuable business asset to a highly specialized performer." Underwriter Jonathan Thomas said, "With his Hollywood clientele it is unlikely that a fake beard could fool children accustomed to seeing their parents transformed into all manner of characters on the silver screen," he said. The face value of his facial hair policy was not disclosed.

In Your Face, Santa!

Clint Westwood, a student at the University of Montana, waited patiently in line for his time with Santa Claus. In front of him a girl about fifteen years of age sat on Santa's lap, but Westwood couldn't wait any longer. He walked up to Santa and "lightly smooshed" a pumpkin pie into the jolly old elf's face. According to a December 1, 2007, AP article, Westwood had a cameraman shoot the entire incident and intended to use it in his documentary film entitled *My Crazy Life*. When the twenty-two-year-old drama student came back to get Santa to sign a release, he was arrested by police on misdemeanor assault charges. "It's a good thing he didn't wait around because I think Santa would have laid him out," said Sergeant Travis Welsh of the Missoula Police Department.

Santa Games

Jim Chan of Hong Kong competed with nine participants during the 2009 Santa Games in Gällivare in northern Sweden, and emerged from the chimney as the number one Santa. According to a November 30, 2009, article in the *Local*, a Swedish newspaper, it was Chan's porridge-eating skills that cinched his red-suited victory. Other events included chimney climbing, present wrapping, and reindeer racing. The Santa Games have been held for the last six years as a part of Gällivare's Snöyran winter festival. Australian David Dawney, the winner of the 2007 Santa Games, prepared for the reindeer competition at home by using his country's most famous animals. "It's a bit bumpy with kangaroos," Dawney told Sveriges Television following a disappointing finish in the reindeer competition. Each contestant in the Santa Games must be "nice to everyone, especially children"; he or she also needs to be "clean and looking their Santa best" and "completely sober." Chan, who doesn't speak Swedish or English, wished everyone a "Merry Christmas!" in his native Cantonese.

Bedford Falls

The warmhearted fantasy *It's a Wonderful Life*, produced and directed by Frank Capra for Liberty Films, was nominated for five Oscars (without winning any) and is recognized by the American Film Institute as one of the one hundred best American films ever made; it is number one on their list of the most inspirational American films of all time. But when it was first released on December 20, 1946, it was considered a "flop." The movie cost $2.3 million and grossed only about $2 million during its initial release—less than half of what Liberty Films expected.

911 CALLER:

"Where can I get rid of my Christmas tree?"

What's in the Window?

In 2009, conceptual artist Keith McGuckin had provocative displays in three separate windows in downtown Oberlin, Ohio. One had Santa in an iron lung sleigh, the second featured a snowman named Norman using old Christmas trees to set fire to a foreclosed home, and in the third, gingerbread men re-created the November 24, 1963, killing of Lee Harvey Oswald by nightclub owner Jack Ruby. In a December 2, 2009, article in the *Elyria Chronicle-Telegram*, McGuckin insisted that his work "The Amazing Iron Lung Santa" is an inspirational tribute to those who suffered from polio in the 1950s and whose lives were saved by the advent of the iron lung. "This is a Santa who, even though he has polio and is in an iron lung, is going to go out and do his job," McGuckin said.

And the Winner Is . . .

The National Liberation Army (Ejército de Liberación Nacional, or ELN) is a revolutionary Marxist guerrilla group that has operated in Colombia since 1964 and is known for violence, kidnapping, and armed attacks. But now they're known for something else: male beauty pageants. A raid in 2003 uncovered a forty-minute video of an ELN Christmas party featuring a mock beauty pageant performed by giddy rebel soldiers wearing only bikini bottoms with sashes across their chests, gleefully strutting down a makeshift catwalk. The beauty contestants were cheered on by an audience of women. The contest was emceed by a ski-masked announcer who proclaimed, in one instance, "Her measurements are round, wide, and built like the back of a horse." According to a September 9, 2003, Reuters article, immediately after the pageant the tape cuts to images of four kidnapped men with their hands bound behind their backs, weakly declaring their ages on camera.

Stocking Stuffers

According to police spokeswoman Kara Winton, shortly before Christmas 2003, Tammi Edwards was caught in a Fort Myers, Florida, store taking four shirts off a rack and insisting that her eleven-year-old daughter stuff them into her handbag. The twenty-nine-year-old Edwards told police that she had intended for the four shirts, valued at fifty-seven dollars, to be Christmas gifts for her daughter. No word on what charges the mother faced, but the young girl, who didn't live with her mom, was referred to a juvenile misdemeanor program.

And Away We Go!

Police in Columbia, South Carolina, arrested a drunken driver after he passed a slow-moving vehicle and sped down Main Street. That doesn't seem like an uncommon occurrence until you find out that the intoxicated man was driving a float in the Anderson, South Carolina, Christmas parade. Forty-two-year-old David Allen Rodgers had an open container of alcohol in his truck that he was using to pull children—including his own child—and adults on a float for a dance studio. Witnesses observed Rodgers pulling out to pass a tractor then racing down Main Street and running a red light. According to a December 20, 2006, AP article, a passenger on the float called 911 to report Rodgers's erratic behavior. Rodgers faced more than three dozen charges, including driving under the influence, kidnapping, and assaulting an officer.

A New "Wrap" Sheet

According to a December 5, 2006, Rock Hill, South Carolina, police report, a twelve-year-old boy was arrested and charged with petty larceny after his mother turned him into the police. The child's crime? He had opened a Christmas present without his mother's permission. The young boy opened a Nintendo Game Boy after being told by family members not to open any gifts until Christmas morning. The twenty-seven-year-old single mother told the *Rock Hill Herald* that her son is disruptive and hoped that the arrest would be the tough love he needed to curb his unruly behavior at home and at school.

Five-Finger Discount

In December 2005, Lucella Bridget Gorman pleaded guilty in Brisbane, Queensland, in Australia, to two counts of theft. The thirty-eight-year-old Banyo, Queensland, woman pleaded guilty to one count of stealing fruit, chocolate, Barbie dolls, toys, batteries, electronics, beauty products, and earrings from a local department store. Her second guilty plea came after police took her mug shot at the station, and Gorman decided to steal the digital camera used by the officer. According to a December 17, 2005, article in Brisbane's *Courier Mail*, after being asked why she stole the merchandise, Gorman claimed, "I didn't have enough money for Christmas and I thought that would be an easy way of getting things."

No, Virginia . . .

Some parents targeted Fabiola Mehu Pelissier, a substitute kindergarten teacher at Forest Hills Elementary School in Coral Springs, Florida, after she let the cat out of the bag concerning Santa Claus. Mehu Pelissier told her class there was no such thing as Santa Claus, and she was quickly reprimanded by assistant principal Lisa George, who urged the teacher to "be more sensitive to holiday traditions." But that slap on the wrist wasn't enough for parent Melissa Shea, who wanted the teacher kicked out of class. "I feel like no matter what I do or say now, the seed of doubt has been planted in [my daughter's] head," complained Shea. As reported on December 14, 2002, in the *South Florida Sun-Sentinel*, the school promised to mend the fantasy by bringing in a Santa "with a natural, full white beard" to "set the record straight" with the kindergarteners.

Sing-a-long

Every December at the Christmas gift market in the northeast England town of North Shields a singing competition is held for children under ten. But according to a September 11, 2002, article in the *Telegraph*, education officers from the North Tyneside Council condemned the contest because the competition might upset the children who didn't win. The organizers of the event, the North Shields Chamber of Trade and Commerce, were told it would be "more acceptable" if held in a noncompetitive form. "Obviously I'm not taking their advice about this. I'm a firm believer in competition," said Maggie Richardson, the president of the North Shields Chamber of Trade and Commerce.

That's How He Rolls!

London-based artist Mark McGowan labeled his performance art "Rollover 2002." McGowan planned to roll—yes, roll—from the Elephant and Castle (a major road intersection in South London, England), across London to an alternative art space called 1,000,000,000 mph in Bethnal Green. McGowen, who worked for two years as a night office cleaner to fund his work, dressed in waterproof pants, a parka, a red knit hat, and rubber gloves and sang "We Wish You a Merry Christmas" to encourage people to be kind to cleaners over the Christmas holiday. McGowan reportedly made no special preparations or did anything to physically prepare for his "roll" in the event. After speaking with the press after a false start, McGowan then rolled and sang for eight and a half hours, finishing bruised, bloodied, dizzy, and feeling "emotional" about his performance.

One-Hit Wonders

Yes, it's sick," McHenry County, Illinois, state's attorney Gary
Pack told the *Chicago Tribune* on November 21, 2002. "But
it's true. We've got two parents here who gave bongs to their kids
for Christmas. I can't believe it either. But it happened." A police
drug raid of a Crystal Lake home of Robert and Theresa Dolin
in 2001 uncovered not only an enormous collection of marijuana
pipes and other drug paraphernalia but some photographs of some
happy recipients of two new Christmas bongs: the Dolins' teenage
children. The photograph shows the Dolin children, sitting under
the Christmas tree, unwrapping their hookahs. Pack said, "It's hard
enough being a teenager without your parents helping you to
become a drug addict." Speculating about what could be under the
tree next year, Pack said, "A gift certificate for a rehab center?"

Lola, L-O-L-A, Lola

Chattanooga, Tennessee, police found and detained a person who was roaming the streets at night, drinking beer and wearing a little girl's dress that he had stolen from under a neighbor's Christmas tree. What makes this story even more disturbing is that the cross-dressing alcoholic was a four-year-old boy. April Wright, the child's twenty-one-year-old mother, said her son "wants to go to jail because that's where his daddy is." According to a December 17, 2009, AP article, the boy was taken to a local hospital and treated for alcohol consumption. Wright said she has already met with child protective services and claims she was told she will get to keep custody of her son.

It's Beginning to Look a Lot Like Christmas

It quickly began being referred to as the "Winter Blunderland," or the less polite "Crapland." A Christmas-themed tourist attraction called Lapland New Forest, on the Dorset-Hampshire border in England, garnered more than 1,300 complaints from disgruntled visitors. Isobel Hollis from Herefordshire, who spent £90 ($130) on rides and attractions as well as £125 ($180) to take her family to the park, described Lapland New Forest as "starving husky dogs, burger vans, two reindeer, a plywood Nativity scene set amongst a muddy scrambler course, tacky market stalls and a fair which charged £2.50 ($3.60) a ride." Another visitor, Wendy Parker, who runs Westhaven preschool in Weymouth, felt "bitterly disappointed" by the tourist destination. "The log cabins were sheds, the Tunnel of Light was a few fairy lights on trees and there was some fake snow sprayed on a few branches." Some visitors went beyond verbal discontent to physical violence. According to a December 3, 2008, article in the *Daily Mail*, furious parents allegedly confronted "elves" in a "gingerbread house," and Father Christmas was punched in the nose by a father who waited in line with his child for four hours before being told he couldn't take his own photograph and that the child wasn't allowed to sit on Santa's lap.

Worse Than Fruitcake

Not sure what to get that certain someone for Christmas? How about a dollop of Donner DNA? That's right, a real blob of Finnish reindeer DNA sealed in a vial adorned with silver antlers. Richard Collins, project manager at Hong Kong–based DNA Tech, Ltd., said interested customers will pay only about sixty-two dollars per sample. "The pendant contains the entire genetic code of a reindeer. So if, in the future, you had the technology, you could, in theory, reproduce a whole reindeer," Collins said in a December 18, 2002, article in the *Chicago Tribune*. "We think it's a nice Christmas gift."

Our Hats Are Off to Them

The garbage collectors, or more colloquially, "binmen," in Kingston upon Hull, in East Yorkshire, England, wore traditional red Santa hats for years. But as reported in a December 9, 2006, article in the *Sun*, the East Yorkshire City Council banned such gay apparel and stated, "Employees can wear Christmas hats in their own time. Wearing them during work time does not create a professional impression." One angry binman said, "Our Santa hats have always brought a bit of festive cheer to local households. We loved seeing the faces of excited kids watching us from the window and laughing at our hats." He added, "It doesn't look like anyone can escape the PC brigade this year."

Saving Christmas One Ornament at a Time

Following the previously mentioned binmen bonnet ban, the *Sun* launched a "Kick 'Em in the Baubles" campaign in December 2006 to prevent killjoys, Grinches, Scrooges, and the well-intentioned politically correct from axing Christmas celebrations around the country. They lost their first battle when health and safety officials in the village of Elstree in the Hertsmere borough of Hertfordshire, England, issued new safety standards for Christmas decorations. The officials announced that Paul Welsh, the town's entertainment officer, "would need to comply with new standards [but] could not upgrade in time." Therefore the town would be without its Christmas lights for the first time in nearly forty years. Fortunately, the *Sun* was able to save Christmas by convincing Job Center area manager Chris Nicol to lift his ban on decorations in his South London offices. One grateful worker exclaimed, "Thanks to the *Sun* we can now have our decorations back." Wow, the power of the press.

It's Muzak to My Ears

Muzak, also known as piped music or elevator music, can be most annoying at times, but it reaches its apex of annoyingness during Christmastime. Endless repeats of "Merry Christmas Everybody," "Santa Claus Is Coming to Town," and "Wonderful Christmastime" can cause the sweetest celebrant to go postal as they are forced to listen to "one of the scourges of modern life." The supermarket giant Sainsbury's, the third largest chain of supermarkets in the United Kingdom, reintroduced piped music over the Christmas period after banning it from their 788 branches in 2006. Nigel Rodgers, of the campaign group Pipe Down, said: "Sainsbury's decision is extremely disappointing and goes against a pledge made by the chief executive himself, Justin King, to drop plans to install piped music. We're not against music, but people don't have a choice but to listen to canned music." According to a December 9, 2007, report in the *Telegraph*, the UK Noise Association conducted a survey of shop workers and found that only 6 percent said they like piped music, 17 percent didn't mind it, 40 percent hated it, and 25 percent tried to ignore it. "It's especially annoying at Christmas when you can walk from one shop to another and hear the same song ten times," Val Weedon, of the UK Noise Association said.

Going Ape for Christmas

A couple brought their pet chimpanzee to the Nicollet Mall in Minneapolis, Minnesota, in 1988 and persuaded Santa Claus to pose with the monkey. But as soon as the camera's flashbulb went off, the chimpanzee went, well, bananas. He tore off Santa's beard, attacked the elf taking the picture, and literally went ape-sh*t (or literally took an ape-sh*t). The Dayton's North Pole, inside the Dayton's store in the mall, had to be closed for an hour to clean up the mess and fumigate the smell.

"Cocaine Dealer Dreaming of a White Christmas"

—JANUARY 24, 2005, REUTERS HEADLINE

Believe

Patricia White Bull, while giving birth to her fourth child in 1983, fell into a catatonic state in which she was unable to speak, swallow, or move much. Her four children were moved from Albuquerque, New Mexico, to the Standing Rock Sioux Reservation in South Dakota to be raised by her husband after doctors told him that his wife would never come out of her coma. But on Christmas Eve, 1999, nursing staff were surprised as they were trying to adjust her bed and White Bull suddenly snapped back into consciousness and complained, "Don't do that!" According to a January 5, 2000, BBC News report, doctors were unable to explain her amazing revitalization but her mother, Snowflake Flower, said it was simply a Christmas miracle from God.

Tug and Chug

Indianapolis police watching the crowd outside Conseco Fieldhouse before an Indiana Pacers game observed a nineteen-year-old woman taking a photo of Santa Claus and then ripping off his beard. The unmasked Father Christmas complained to police because the beard had been glued to his face, and the quick removal caused him a great deal of discomfort. Officers followed the beard-busting woman inside the arena and discovered she had a bottle of vodka hidden under her shirt. The December 22, 2009, issue of the *Indianapolis Star* reported that police arrested the woman and two others on charges of public intoxication and possession of alcohol by a minor.

Like a Bowl Full of Sugar-Free Nonfat Jelly

A very fit Father Christmas is refusing to wear stuffing under his red suit because he doesn't want to promote childhood obesity. Bill Winton, a petite, 168-pound, eighty-year-old Santa said if children idolized a corpulent Kris Kringle they might grow up believing that it's OK to be chubby. "The parents and kids have been asking why I'm so thin and I say 'Santa's been on a diet.'" Winton, who has noticed that children sitting on his knee are getting heavier and heavier said, "I have always eaten healthily and have run a healthy-eating course in the past. I gave up cola years ago when I saw what it did to a penny." According to a December 17, 2007, article in the *Telegraph* Winton, hoped that "Other Santas across the country follow suit so that parents start taking responsibility for their children's diets." And in a not-so-jolly final thought, he exclaimed, ere he drove out of sight, "It makes me wonder why parents allow their children to get into that state and makes me slightly annoyed about it."

Almost Nicked Nick

He wasn't using his reindeer to fly this time, which is good, because Rudolph might have been capped. As reported in the *New York Times* on December 19, 2007, a Santa Claus flying in a helicopter and carrying toys to give to children in a Rio de Janeiro slum was fired upon by suspected drug traffickers. Mistaking the jolly old elf for a police operative, the drug traffickers hit the helicopter twice and forced the copper to return to base. But Santa, undaunted, substituted reindeer power for horsepower and took a car to complete his mission.

Clean Your Mouth Out with Soap

In 2006, Microsoft encouraged kids to chat with "Santa" by adding northpole@live.com to their Windows Live Messenger contact lists. They reactivated the bot program in early December 2007. Santa asked children what they wanted for Christmas, and he was able to respond on topic thanks to artificial intelligence. But they don't call it artificial intelligence for nothing. Microsoft quickly shut down the program when two girls told their uncle that Santa had made rude comments to them after they asked him to eat a slice of pizza. The Register, a UK technology site, picked up on the story and ran a test of the Microsoft Santa bot. When they asked Santa to eat a slice of pizza he responded, "You want me to eat what?!? It's fun to talk about oral sex, but I want to chat about something else." According to a December 6, 2007, AP article, the exchange between the Register writer and Santa ended with them calling each other "dirty bastard."

Not as Jolly as He Used to Be

The stump of a pipe he held tight in his teeth,
And the smoke it encircled his head like a wreath.

But not in the special eight-week Santa Claus training course in Weston-super-Mare College in England, according to an August 2, 1998, article in the *Independent.* "They will have to learn that children are little adults and should be treated with respect," the course tutor, who spoke only on condition of anonymity, said. "You cannot have Father Christmas drinking or smoking—I constantly suck breath fresheners," said the tutor. The college is also planning to organize a national coalition for qualified Santas.

One Good Turn
Deserves Another

In March 2000, forty-seven-year-old Christina Lowman went to the local Humane Society in Home, Pennsylvania, and adopted a terrier-mix dog who was recovering from an accident that had cost him his right hind leg and severed his tail. She named the pooch Percy, and since she basically saved his life, he returned the favor on Christmas morning of the same year. Lowman had just stepped outside in the eleven-degree weather when she slipped on an icy ramp and was knocked unconscious. According to a January 1, 2001, article in the *Pittsburgh Post-Gazette*, Lowman, who had no idea how long she had been lying in the freezing weather, said she was roused out of her state of unconsciousness by Percy, who was licking her face and barking at her. Lowman credits Percy with a Christmas miracle because she knows she would have died in the frigid weather if it weren't for her three-legged, tailless mutt.

All Hail Christmas

Rossmann, a chain of health, perfumeries, and beauty shops that has more than 2,100 stores in Germany, Poland, Hungary, and the Czech Republic, decided to remove miniature wooden Santa Claus figurines from its shelves after readers of the daily tabloid *Bild* saw pictures of them. The Santa figures wore a silly red hat with a white pom-pom, carried a bag of toys, and raised their right arms toward the sky. What's wrong with that? Well, according to a December 2, 2006, article in the *New York Times*, it looks for all the world like Santa is giving everyone the Nazi salute—especially when there are rows of Santas. It is against the law in Germany to perform the Nazi salute, also called the Hitler salute. The producer of the figures, Haymann, was surprised by the reaction. "It looks like they're just pointing up to the sky," the company told *Bild*.

The Final Flight

The Danish Air Force paid damages to Santa Claus after one of its low-flying fighter jets accidentally killed Rudolph. Olovi Nikkanoff, who lives on the central Danish island of Fyn and portrayed Santa Claus, officially complained to the Danish Air Force after a veterinarian concluded that Nikkanoof's reindeer had had a heart attack from the shock of the deafening noise made by the fighter plane. According to a September 29, 2005, article in the *New York Times*, the Danish Air Force agreed to pay Nikkanoff 30,000 kroner ($4,840) to buy a replacement Rudolph.

I Thought He Had a Red Nose?

I had to listen to it three times. I thought it was a skip, but then I heard it," said Frank Ehrhardt, assistant manager of a Welland, Ontario, retail store. What he and others heard was an obscene version of "Rudolph the Red-Nosed Reindeer" coming from six-inch singing Santa figurines. The lyrics were, in part: "Rudolph, the red-nosed dickhead, has a shiny nose that blows," sang in a voice similar to the late Burl Ives. According to a December 17, 1998, Reuters article, the Canadian Tire Corp., Ltd., pulled the dirty Santas from their shelves and offered a refund to anyone who had purchased the twenty-dollar item. The glitch was likely caused by "someone at the manufacturing plant [in China] having a bad night," Ehrhardt said.

Art for Art's Sake

I want people to say 'Oh, my gosh,'" said window artist Keith McGuckin. "And once they look at it, say, 'It is kind of pretty.'" But Charlie Palmer, the owner of the store in Oberlin, Ohio, said that "A few of his other displays were on the edge. But never that crazy." The Christmas display in question featured, in one window, gingerbread men dressed as Nazi storm troopers. Another window had a snow woman sitting under a hair dryer in an apparent suicide attempt. McGurkin defended his Nazi-themed Christmas display by saying, "I can differentiate between real Nazis and the atrocities they performed compared to these little gingerbread men, but I guess some people can't." According to a December 15, 2006, article in the *Elyria Chronicle-Telegram*, McGuckin's display at the store the previous year included a little boy making crystal meth using his new chemistry set.

I Thought I Was Tiny Tim

Maybe Santa, not Grandma, got run over by a reindeer—but whatever the reason, Santa, many Santas in fact, were seen hobbling around with crutches and bandaged legs at the Value City in Covington, Kentucky, as part of a slightly strange holiday marketing campaign for the chain of discount stores. As reported in the December 20, 2003, *New York Times*, the fractured Father Christmases were the idea of New York advertising agency Cliff Freeman & Partners. The crippled Clauses handed out coupons good for ten dollars off any purchase of fifty dollars or more and gave away cards, resembling handwritten notes, that read: "I hurt myself during chimney practice, so I won't be able to help you with gifts this year. Please use this Value City coupon in my absence." Some people thought the campaign was cute but others, such as Jim Silver, publisher of *Toy Wishes* magazine, said, "I think it's terrible. I don't want my five-year-old to feel sorry for Santa."

A Brewing Controversy

The Liquor Control Division of Hartford, Connecticut, notified Shelton Brothers distributors that they were rejecting its application to sell a certain brand of beer. Was the alcohol content too high? Was the beer contaminated? Nope, its label featured a mean-looking elf shooting ornaments at Santa's sleigh with a slingshot. Seriously Bad Elf is a bitter winter ale brewed at the Ridgeway Brewery in England and distributed by the Shelton Brothers, but state liquor regulations said it's illegal for alcohol advertising to use images that might appeal to children. According to an October 29, 2006, AP article, Dan Shelton, owner of Shelton Brothers, complained that his company had had no complaints when it sold Bad Elf and Very Bad Elf in previous years, nor had they registered any complaints in any of the thirty states in which they sell beer. "The state of Connecticut must not have enough to think about," said Gary A. Lippincott, the Massachusetts artist responsible for the image on the beer's label.

Torch Song

How can you have a torchlight procession with glow sticks? We'll be the laughingstock of the county," complained John Andrews, who helps organize the annual nighttime Christmas torchlight procession in Looe, Cornwall, in England. Government officials told organizers that they had to replace the traditional torches with glow sticks because of the risk of fire or an accident. The event, which had taken place since 1985 and attracted nearly five hundred participants, had never had any injury or fire damage of any kind. Nevertheless, according to a November 19, 2005, UPI News Service article, government officials feared that their town would be sued if there were an accident stemming from the use of torches. "It's an absolute joke," said Andrews. But the show went on, and in lieu of torches, organizers paid about $600 for five hundred glow sticks.

Santa versus the Terrorists

S eptember eleventh really is the Grinch that stole Christmas,"
said sixty-three-year-old Maurice De Witt of New York, New
York. De Witt, who portrayed Santa Claus, noticed a marked
difference in how people related to him and he reacted to other
people following the terrorist attacks. "Now, I get a little afraid
when someone comes to touch me, or gets too close," he said. "I'm
afraid they might rub something on me, trying to get the kids sick
or something." Quoted in a September 11, 2002, article in the
New York Times, De Witt said he had worked one month a year in
front of Rockefeller Center as a Santa with Volunteers of America
for the previous eight years. He said he hadn't lost his faith in the
season but was disappointed in the parents of the children and, in a
small way, in himself.

You're on *Candid Camera*

*Y*es, I've been a bad girl," said Virginia Voiers of Eureka Springs, Arkansas. Voiers was ticketed for misdemeanor theft after a surveillance camera caught her stealing . . . the Baby Jesus. "It was a lark, it wasn't any serious stealing," Voiers told the *Lovely County Citizen* on December 3, 2005. "My granddaughter commented that no one had taken the Baby Jesus this year and said, 'Grandma?' I said, 'Oh, what the heck.'" Voiers, who is seventy years old and a Sunday school teacher at a Methodist church, said she told her pastor what happened. "He said, 'Bless you, child. Go and sin no more,'" Voiers reported, adding that he asked, "You didn't tell them you are a Methodist, did you?" Police chief Earl Hyatt said he was taking the case seriously and considered charging the septuagenarian with theft, which carries a possible penalty of a year in jail and $1,000 fine.

Stealing the Baby Jesus isn't Eureka Springs' only Christmas tradition, reported a December 3, 2005, article in the *Arkansas Democrat-Gazette*. Former mayor Beau Satori says that in the past, someone was rearranging the animals in the Nativity scene into "uncompromising positions."

Charlie Brown's Tree Is "Third-Class"

Is your Christmas tree "first-class" or "third-class"? Didn't know Christmas trees had a class system? Well, they do in Norway. In an October 13, 1998, Reuters article, Finn Hjalmar Andersen, spokesman of the Norwegian Standards Association, said starting immediately Norway Christmas trees were to be standardized, as part of a battle to curb imports from neighboring Denmark. A "first-class" tree is straight with a single tip, a regular shape and color, is free of artificial insecticides or fertilizers, and must be felled after November 20 (with a label proving date of harvest). Trees with curved trucks or uneven branches would be rated "third-class." The association sets standards for products from food packaging to bicycle safety helmets and in 1999 set guidelines for earthquake-proof buildings—even though quakes hardly ever happen in Norway.

Christmas Is Too Commercial

Although Santa Claus has been used in commercial advertising for years (in fact, the modern appearance of Santa Claus was a commercial creation of Coca-Cola), not all commercial endeavors work as intended. According to a November 24, 2000, *New York Times* article, Sony executives pulled the plug on an elaborate television campaign before the first commercial hit the air for fear that they would be misinterpreted by the viewing audience. The first of the four commercials, designed to be run in sequence, showed Santa being kidnapped; the second showed him blindfolded and stumbling around; the third showed golf balls being hit at him; and the fourth spot showed Santa released only to find his car covered with parking tickets. The campaign, by the advertising firm of Young & Rubicam, was for SonyStyle.com, a Web site that sells Sony Electronics products. Liz Reilly, a spokeswoman for Y&R, said, "Our feeling is that while we knew that these ads pushed the envelope and were edgy, based on the market that we were trying to go to, they were appropriate."

Fur-Lined Collar

Police have been known to be rough on some suspects—even when the suspect is Saint Nick. Salvatore Gonzalez, who was dressed as Santa Claus and leading a group of carolers outside a restaurant holiday party for the disabled, was approached by police after a neighbor complained about the singing. "He threw me against the wall," Gonzalez said, "and he was grabbing me by the Santa suit, and he was shaking me." Gonzalez reported that the singing had stopped before he was even approached by District of Columbia police. The restaurant's owner, Karen Audia Shannon, said, "You would have thought they were collaring a murder suspect. They were a little rough." According to a December 15, 1999, article in the *New York Times*, police arrested Gonzalez and charged him with disorderly conduct.

The True Spirit of Christmas

For at least twenty years, Elmer Buller had played Santa in the Mountain Lake community, about one hundred miles southwest of Minneapolis, Minnesota. But on November 21, 1988, Buller was burned over 25 percent of his body when he fell into a pit of burning coals at Balzer Manufacturing, a manufacturer and distributor of livestock manure and municipal waste—handling equipment, where he served as the custodian. The December 6, 1988, edition of the *New York Times* reported that area children gave Santa Claus a Christmas present that year. The students at Mountain Lake Elementary School made donations to help pay Buller's medical expenses instead of spending their money to exchange presents among themselves. The sixty-year-old Buller, who arrived in full Santa suit in a sleigh or behind a team of horses every year, spent Christmas 1988 in intensive care and told his wife that he would "miss the kids."

Hats Off for Christmas

Twenty-three employees of the Okonite Company, an electrical cable manufacturer in North Brunswick, New Jersey, were suspended without pay shortly before Christmas in 1987. It wasn't because of improper work efforts but because of improper work apparel: They were wearing traditional Santa Claus hats on the job. As a sign of solidarity, one hundred other workers also donned red hats with white trim, and they, too, were promptly suspended. According to a December 23, 1987, AP article, the company released a statement saying that the hats were "carnival-like headwear" inappropriate "for a business environment." The workers returned to work the next day with a little less holiday spirit and without their Christmas chapeaus.

Early Discharge

Dickson Womack, a deputy sheriff posing as an elf at the Santa Fe, New Mexico, state penitentiary, was escorting Santa Claus into the facility to meet children of the inmates. As Womack was unloading his .25-caliber pistol to store it away, it accidentally discharged. The *New York Times* reported on December 26, 1986, that before James Stevenson, who was posing as Santa Claus, could greet the first child he was winged by the bullet.

WARNING LABEL ON A BOX OF CHRISTMAS LIGHTS:
"For indoor or outdoor use only."

What, No Chimney?

An Eastchester, New York, woman was sexually assaulted and robbed by a man who gained entry to the woman's home by telling her he was a firefighter, reported the *New York Times* on December 6, 1985. An Eastchester police spokesman, Detective David Speidell, said the twenty-four-year-old woman explained that she was home alone at about 4:45 p.m. when the man knocked on her door and told her he was raising funds for the Eastchester Fire Department. When she allowed him inside, he pulled out his gun, assaulted her, stole several pieces of jewelry, and fled the premises. The woman claimed she allowed the man to enter her house because he was dressed as Santa Claus.

Ring In Christmas

Pacific Bell Telephone Company in San Francisco, California, set up a special Santa Claus line in 1984 and encouraged children to call Santa. What the phone company didn't promote was that every call cost fifty cents. Lawyers for two children filed a class-action suit for $10 million against the phone company for deceptive advertising. Seven-year-old Josie Aaronson-Gelb told the Associated Press on March 28, 1985, that all her friends were calling Santa Claus on the special number that December, so she called him, too, a total of forty-five times before Christmas. Jack Saunders, a spokesman for Pacific Bell, claimed that under California Public Utilities Commission rules, the company's only responsibilities were to provide a working line and to clearly advertise the cost of each call. The lawsuit sought a refund for the estimated 100,000 families as well as $10 million in punitive damages (and we all know who got those Christmas goodies).

A Real Pearl

Twenty-five-year-old Brian Pearl of Essex, Vermont, was arrested and charged with trespassing after he yelled at children in line to see Santa Claus at the Burlington Square Mall. Pearl, who calls himself a fundamentalist Christian, screamed at the children and toddlers that there was "no such thing" as Santa Claus. District judge Linda Levitt offered to release Pearl on the condition that "he would not return to the mall and would not harass any other Santas," but he said he could not promise to comply. "I think he was acting out of religious principles," the judge said. According to a December 17, 1984, AP article, Pearl, who pleaded not guilty to the trespassing charge, was held on fifty dollars bail.

Going Out with a Bang!

He was arrested for having hoax devices and for making terrorist threats and was held without bond in the Clayton County jail. Forty-five-year-old William C. Caldwell III waited in line at the Southlake Mall in suburban Atlanta, Georgia, for his turn to have his picture taken with Santa Claus. What's odd is that even though Caldwell was not part of the mall's Christmas staff he was dressed as an elf. When he approached Santa, he told him he was carrying dynamite in his bag. The *Chicago Tribune* reported on December 4, 2009, that Santa called mall security, the mall was evacuated, and Caldwell was arrested. Police have no idea what Caldwell's motives were in threatening Santa Claus.

A Taxi Situation

Two men hurriedly jumped into a taxi in Market Harborough, Leicestershire, in England, and screamed at the driver to make a speedy getaway. The taxi driver was about to do what his passengers said and then looked into the rearview mirror and saw why they were in such a hurry: They were being chased by twenty-two men, all dressed as Santa Claus. Before the driver could put the car into gear, the gang of Father Christmases attacked the cab, smashed the rear window, and tried to yank the passengers out. According to an October 29, 2009, article in the *Mirror*, the driver sped away to safety and later claimed that the bizarre incident wouldn't stop him from driving his hack. "I think the chances of being mobbed by a gang of drunken Santas a second time must be very rare," he said.

Drop In Anytime

Reuters reported on January 5, 1993, that Lawrence and Margie Beavers of Oceanside, California, were woken early in the morning by loud groaning coming from their living room. Fifty-six-year-old Margie ran downstairs and found a very stuck Frank Morales hanging upside down in their fireplace, his chest and arms hanging out onto the fire grate but his legs still stuck in the flue. "What are you doing in there?" she asked. "I'm Santa Claus," replied Morales. "So I asked him, 'Where are my gifts?'" Police and firefighters had to chip away at the fireplace until the forty-two-year-old burglary suspect was finally freed—well, until they took him to jail, that is. "After telling the couple he was Santa Claus he explained to them he had dived down their chimney to get away from a group of men who were chasing him. Neither story was very plausible," a police spokesman said. The couple took a photograph of themselves alongside the upside-down burglar and planned to use it as their next Christmas card.

Will the Real Santa Please Stand Up?

Mfter [December 5] Santa is welcome, but until then we don't want him," said Lodewijk Osse, of the Assen Sinterklaas town committee. This small town in the northern Netherlands is protesting Santa Claus and many other familiar Christmas symbols in an attempt to preserve the traditional Dutch Father Christmas, called Sinterklaas, who visits children on December 5, not December 25. It is illegal to sing Christmas carols, shops have posted "No entry for reindeer" signs in their windows, and local police have been granted the authority to arrest visiting Santas and lock them up overnight. According to a November 29, 1994, Reuters article, the townspeople want to preserve the more authentic customs of Christmas and not allow the American "import."

Santa's Aids

Mark Woodley, a former department store Santa Claus, filed suit against Macy's in 1989 after he claimed the store fired him when they found out he had tested HIV positive. According to a December 1, 1991, *New York Daily News* article, the forty-two-year-old Woodley lost his legal fight to reclaim his job for that year's holiday season. As a sign of protest, nineteen AIDS activists, all dressed as Santa, picketed the chain's flagship store in Herald Square and were arrested. A spokesman for Macy's denied the allegations but never clarified why Woodley was kicked out of the North Pole.

Two nineteen-year-olds in Saginaw, Michigan, were cited for underage drinking on December 14, 2000, after they were hunted down by the owner of a snowman they had just hacked apart with swords.

A Lap around the World

The *Chicago Tribune* reported on September 3, 2006, that there was standing room only for a larger-than-expected crowd that turned out for a seminar titled "Santa Ethics." The course helped prospective Santas learn such things as proper placement of hands when they hug a child and whether it's Santa's job to discipline an unruly elf. The Q&A portion of the seminar went from the joys of "ho, ho, ho-ing" to the question of dealing with homosexuals who want to sit on Santa's lap. The nearly overwhelming decision was that all people are children of God and are therefore entitled to sit on Santa's lap. However, when the topic turned from gays and lesbians to allowing members of the Ku Klux Klan to sit on Santa's lap, the room exploded in heated debate.

Cherish Is the Word

Debra Stutts, the mother of Green Bay, Wisconsin, kindergartner Cherish Stutts, said she would homeschool her daughter after a teacher violated the girl's rights. The incident occurred after Cherish started telling other students that Santa Claus wasn't real, and the teacher took her aside and asked her to keep her skepticism about Santa to herself. Cherish claims no one was offended by her statements, but the teacher said she took Cherish aside only after several kindergarteners came to her in tears. In a December 9, 1989, article in the *Milwaukee Sentinel*, Stutts said she would have sued the school if she had enough money to file a lawsuit. The school principal, Graydon Axtell, said he supported the teacher's decision to reprimand the young existentialist.

A Lucky Christmas Ham

The traditional pre-Christmas swine slaughter in the village of Darvaspuszta, in southwestern Hungary, was a stunning failure when two people died during the celebration. An unnamed Croatian man accidentally electrocuted himself with a homemade pig stunner, and the pig's owner was so upset over the incident that he suffered a fatal heart attack. The article didn't report on the fate of the pig.

For Whom the Bell Tolls

An allegedly drunk Salvation Army Christmas bell ringer collecting money for the charity got into a fight with employees at a Safeway store in Denver, Colorado. Forty-six-year-old David Duncan was taken into custody after a routine background check found he had eleven outstanding warrants for his arrest; nine of the eleven warrants were for public consumption of alcohol and two were for trespassing, police detective Teresa Garcia said. In a December 24, 2004, FOX News article, Salvation Army spokeswoman Becky O'Guin was quoted as saying, "Had we known about these outstanding warrants, we would never have hired him."

Plunging into Christmas

A December 24, 2005, AP article reported that Tom Suica, a plumber and Democratic candidate for councilman in Monaca, Pennsylvania, had, since 1999, had his roof decorated with ten toilets as a protest against a bank's plan to build a parking lot next to his home. Barbara Suica did not initially appreciate her husband's protest, nor did Suica's neighbors. He received a letter demanding that the toilets come down because they could be a breeding ground for mosquitoes and West Nile virus. However, Suica convinced the town that his toilets were not a hazard, as he had taped down the covers to keep water from coming in. Suica successfully argued in court that the toilets are covered by the First Amendment and that they are simply decorations. He routinely decorated them at Christmas by mounting antlers on them and installing a Santa Claus cutout. Barbara Suica said, "They're decorated now. I'm not taking down my Christmas decorations."

A Rose by Any Other Name

I pass out love and happiness and the hopes for a better tomorrow," said Kris Kringel in a December 15, 1999, telephone interview with the Associated Press. Kringel, dressed in his famous red and white outfit, lived at the North Pole and delivered wonderful things to people every day: pizza. You see, this Kris Kringel (his real name), was a pizza delivery driver for the Pizza Hut franchise in North Pole, Alaska (population 1,500). Every year at Christmastime, in keeping with his name, he dressed the part. He always physically looked the part, with a long natural beard and a portly belly. Unlike the real Santa Claus, however, this Kringel doesn't work on Christmas Day because the store is closed. In the interview, Kringel said he planned to spend the day in a hot tub at a nearby mineral spring.

Something Extra in Your Stocking

In 2000, the polling institute Forsa in Berlin found that a lot of women wanted something naughty, not nice, for Christmas— an extramarital fling. The data uncovered that women, more than men, hoped their Christmas dream came true at the annual Christmas party. This is not a new idea. In previous research, 7 percent of women said they "regularly" used office parties to be unfaithful to their partners, while only 1 percent of men said they did so.

Off the Rack

S tephen McKittrick and Sean McNeilly spoke to the Liverpool
City Magistrates Court in England during their five-minute
hearing to confirm their names, addresses, and dates of birth before
being remanded on unconditional bail to appear before the same
court on January 9, 2001. The two men, according to a December
2000 AP article, were arrested on charges of "undertaking or
assisting in the retention or removal of stolen goods." McKittrick
and McNeilly had been caught red-handed stealing red and white
Santa suits.

Special Delivery

On Christmas Day one might expect to look into the sky and see Santa Claus descending with his team of reindeer, but on one particular Christmas Day, an airport worker instead saw the body of seventeen-year-old Alberto Vazquez Rodriguez. Rodriguez had apparently been a stowaway in the undercarriage of a British Airways plane en route to Mexico from London. The body of another Cuban military school cadet, sixteen-year-old Maikel Fonseca Almira, was found in a field directly under a flight path for both Gatwick Airport and Heathrow on Christmas Eve. Reuters reported on December 26, 2001, that a note left by one of the boys indicated they were attempting to reach the United States.

King Baby

"Parents are increasingly demanding that we bring the stick and scold their kids rather than deliver the goodies," complained Joerg Rupert Schoepfel in a December 24, 2001, interview with the German tabloid *Bild*. Schoephfel, who runs a rent-a-Santa service that dispatches hundreds of students dressed as Father Christmas, has noticed a marked difference in the parents of today. "When kids wet their beds, it's not a problem I should have to deal with." Schoephfel said that parents want to use Santa Claus as leverage to make them behave more like little adults. He said many parents want him and his hundreds of part-time Santas to chastise their children into working harder in school, to stop fighting with their siblings, to clean up after themselves, to clean up their rooms, and to stop sucking their thumbs or pacifiers. "I'm tired of having to take their pacifiers with me," he said. "I've got at least fifty already."

The Proof of the Pudding Is in the Eating

According to a December 18, 1990, article in the *Wall Street Journal*, the Wilkinsons, a family in Sussex, England, received a gift from their Australian relatives that they assumed was a package of herbs for a traditional Christmas pudding. They merrily mixed up the dough, baked the pudding, ate half of it, and then placed the other half in the refrigerator. Reported the *Journal*, "Soon thereafter, a member of the family relates, 'We heard from Auntie Sheila that Uncle Eric had died, and had we received his ashes for burial in Britain.' Shocked, the Wilkinsons quickly summoned a vicar to bless, and bury, Uncle Eric's leftovers."

Too Nice for His
Own Good

Retired Marine pilot Al Maiern, from Laguna Beach, California, served six months in jail primarily because he had too many old cars parked in the driveway of his house. According to police records from 1991, Maiern was also jailed for allowing a homeless family to live, free of charge, in the spare bedroom of his house. Frank Battaile, deputy city attorney for Laguna Beach, explained, "Mr. Maier is known for supposedly doing charitable things and being the Laguna Beach Santa Claus. But his neighbors complained about property values."

Tell Santa What You Think

Todd Tokarz of Gages Lake, Illinois, about forty-five miles north of Chicago, was working as the town Santa Claus when he was caught telling children not to say the traditional word "cheese" when smiling for the camera. "He was working that day as the resident Santa at Lakehurst and was apparently telling little kids, as they were posing for the camera, to say 'school sucks,'" said assistant state's attorney George Strickland. According to a December 22, 1995, *Chicago Tribune* article, Tokarz was arrested after a routine background check showed that he had outstanding warrants for aggravated criminal abuse and criminal sexual assault after allegedly forcing a fifteen-year-old girl to have sex, Strickland said.

Liquor Is Quicker

We're going to run a test project to see if the whey can be distilled," Halvor Heuch, master blender at the Norwegian alcohol group Arcus, explained to Independent Online, on August 12, 2002. The firm was attempting to make Santa a little jollier that year by distilling alcohol from the whey left over after making cheese from reindeer milk. The test would be run on twenty-one deer, from which the company would produce cheese and then hopefully reindeer rum. Heuch said he doubted if any reindeer alcohol could win a big market, even if the test were successful: "This is unlikely to be anything more than a curiosity," he said.

Up in Smoke

Every year in the Swedish city of Gävle, the oldest city in Sweden's historical Northern Lands (Norrland), Swedes filled with Christmas cheer celebrate by building a gigantic straw Yule Goat. And every year, Christmas Scrooge Swedes respond by burning the highly combustible icon to the ground. According to a December 25, 2009, article in the *San Francisco Chronicle*, the first Yule Goat was built in 1966 and was quickly followed by the first burning of the Yule Goat. On occasions the Yule Goat has also been shredded, amputated, and mutilated before being torched.

Don't Drop a Log

The Caga Tió is a fixture in Spanish Christmas traditions and can be equated to a slightly perverted piñata. Caga Tió, which translates to "pooping log," is a small log with a drawn or applied face, little legs, and usually a cape of some kind. In early December, the adults in a household will "feed" the log by putting in small treats such as hazelnuts or small pieces of chocolate. Then, on Christmas Day, the children joyously gather around the Caga Tió and beat it with sticks until it drops its load through a small hole in its underside. On December 25, 2009, the *San Francisco Chronicle* featured a traditional song that accompanies the beating of the Caga Tió:

> *Poop turrón [sweet nougat candy],*
> *Hazelnuts and cottage cheese,*
> *If you don't poop well,*
> *I'll hit you with a stick,*
> *Poop log!*
> *Poop log!*
> *Log of Christmas,*
> *Don't poop herrings,*
> *Which are too salty,*
> *Poop turrón*
> *Which is much better!*